Research Series on the Chinese Dream and China's Development Path

Project Director

Xie Shouguang, President, Social Sciences Academic Press

Series Editors

Li Yang, Chinese Academy of Social Sciences, Beijing, China
Li Peilin, Chinese Academy of Social Sciences, Beijing, China

Academic Advisors

Cai Fang, Gao Peiyong, Li Lin, Li Qiang, Ma Huaide, Pan Jiahua, Pei Changhong, Qi Ye, Wang Lei, Wang Ming, Zhang Yuyan, Zheng Yongnian, Zhou Hong

Drawing on a large body of empirical studies done over the last two decades, this Series provides its readers with in-depth analyses of the past and present and forecasts for the future course of China's development. It contains the latest research results made by members of the Chinese Academy of Social Sciences. This series is an invaluable companion to every researcher who is trying to gain a deeper understanding of the development model, path and experience unique to China. Thanks to the adoption of Socialism with Chinese characteristics, and the implementation of comprehensive reform and opening-up, China has made tremendous achievements in areas such as political reform, economic development, and social construction, and is making great strides towards the realization of the Chinese dream of national rejuvenation. In addition to presenting a detailed account of many of these achievements, the authors also discuss what lessons other countries can learn from China's experience.

More information about this series at http://www.springer.com/series/13571

Yiming Yuan
Editor

Studies on China's Special Economic Zones 3

Editor
Yiming Yuan
China Center for Special Economic Zones
Shenzhen University
Shenzhen, Guangdong, China

ISSN 2363-6866   ISSN 2363-6874   (electronic)
Research Series on the Chinese Dream and China's Development Path
ISBN 978-981-13-9843-8   ISBN 978-981-13-9841-4   (eBook)
https://doi.org/10.1007/978-981-13-9841-4

Jointly published with Social Sciences Academic Press
The print edition is not for sale in China. Customers from China please order the print book from: Social
Sciences Academic Press.

This Springer imprint is published by the registered company Springer Nature Singapore Pte Ltd.
The registered company address is: 152 Beach Road, #21-01/04 Gateway East, Singapore 189721,
Singapore

Series Preface

Since China's reform and opening began in 1978, the country has come a long way on the path of socialism with Chinese characteristics, under the leadership of the Communist Party of China. Over 30 years of reform, efforts and sustained spectacular economic growth have turned China into the world's second largest economy and wrought many profound changes in the Chinese society. These historically significant developments have been garnering increasing attention from scholars, governments, and the general public alike around the world since the 1990s, when the newest wave of China studies began to gather steam. Some of the hottest topics have included the so-called China miracle, Chinese phenomenon, Chinese experience, Chinese path, and the Chinese model. Homegrown researchers have soon followed suit. Already hugely productive, this vibrant field is putting out a large number of books each year, with Social Sciences Academic Press alone having published hundreds of titles on a wide range of subjects.

Because most of these books have been written and published in Chinese, however, readership has been limited outside China—even among many who study China—for whom English is still the lingua franca. This language barrier has been an impediment to efforts by academia, business communities, and policy-makers in other countries to form a thorough understanding of contemporary China, of what is distinct about China's past and present may mean not only for her future but also for the future of the world. The need to remove such an impediment is both real and urgent, and the *Research Series on the Chinese Dream and China's Development Path* is my answer to the call.

This series features some of the most notable achievements from the last 20 years by scholars in China in a variety of research topics related to reform and opening. They include both theoretical explorations and empirical studies and cover economy, society, politics, law, culture, and ecology, the six areas in which reform and opening policies have had the deepest impact and farthest reaching consequences for the country. Authors for the series have also tried to articulate their visions of the "Chinese Dream" and how the country can realize it in these fields and beyond.

All of the editors and authors for the *Research Series on the Chinese Dream and China's Development Path* are both longtime students of reform and opening and recognized authorities in their respective academic fields. Their credentials and expertise lend credibility to these books, each of which having been subject to a rigorous peer-review process for inclusion in the series. As part of the Reform and Development Program under the State Administration of Press, Publication, Radio, Film, and Television of the People's Republic of China, the series is published by Springer, a Germany-based academic publisher of international repute and distributed overseas. I am confident that it will help fill a lacuna in studies of China in the era of reform and opening.

Xie Shouguang

Sponsor and Commitee

Founded in: November, 2008

Sponsor

Key Research Base for Humanities and Social Sciences of Ministry of Education, P. R. China
Center for Special Economic Zone Research, Shenzhen University

Editor-in-chief: Yiming Yuan

Assistant Editor-in-chief: Yikun Zhou

Academic Committee

Chairman: Zhong Wu
Vice Chairmen: Yitao Tao, Anshan You

Members

Anshan You, Shanghai Academy of Social Sciences
Susheng Wang, Harbin Institute of Technology
Qiusheng Tian, South China University of Technology
Zhong Wu, Shenzhen Academy of Social Sciences
Fei Li, Xiamen University
Shenglan Li, Sun Yat-Sen University
Chaolin Wu, South China Normal University

Contents

Chapter 1
The Poverty Reduction Effect of China's Special Economic Zones—Case Study of Shenzhen

Yuan Yiming and He Lei

Abstract There are three kinds of controversial views on the income distribution effect of FDI: the introduction of FDI widens the gap among different regions and the income gap of residents, thus being not conducive to poverty reduction; FDI is conducive to narrowing the gap between the rich and the poor and reducing poverty; and FDI has uncertain effects on income distribution, which are related to the quality of FDI, developmental stage and market environment. This paper conducts a case study of the Shenzhen Special Economic Zone for investigating the effects of the introduction of FDI on the employment of the poor population at the developmental stages of different industries and further exploring the poverty reduction effect of FDI. The results of the empirical analysis show that the FDI industries in different developmental periods are characterized by the changes from labor-intensive to capital- and technology-intensive. In this process, their effect on the employment of the low-income labor force has declined and the function of comprehensive poverty reduction has weakened.

Keywords Special economic zone · FDI · Industrial transformation · Employment

In the past 30 years, Shenzhen has changed from a frontier fishing village to the fastest growing city in China by virtue of its geographical proximity to Hong Kong and Macao and the policy effect of the special economic zone (SEZ). It is also a city with the most concentrated and fastest increasing foreign direct investments. As of 2009, Shenzhen has utilized a total of US$62.77 billion in foreign investments, including US$6.675 billion in foreign borrowings, US$45.63 billion in Foreign Direct Investment (FDI), and US$10.47 billion in other foreign investments. Foreign investments have an effect on the economy of Shenzhen through various transmission mechanisms such as providing capital, technology spillovers, industrial evolution and institutional changes, thus making important contributions to the economic take-off and development of Shenzhen.

Y. Yiming (✉) · H. Lei
China Center for Special Economic Zone Research, Shenzhen University, Shenzhen 518060, Guangdong, China
e-mail: 1033936970@qq.com

© Social Sciences Academic Press 2020
Y. Yuan (ed.), *Studies on China's Special Economic Zones 3*,
Research Series on the Chinese Dream and China's Development Path,
https://doi.org/10.1007/978-981-13-9841-4_1

Experience shows that FDI plays an obvious role of promotion and makes a great contribution to the economic growth of Shenzhen. However, economic development does not necessarily lead to improvement of income distribution and reduction of the number of people living in poverty. In comparison with domestic investments, FDI, as a kind of capital investment, has obvious differences in the effect mechanisms of overall economic development and income distribution, and thus it has different effects on poverty reduction. With a case study of Shenzhen, this paper examines the effect of FDI on promoting Shenzhen's economic development and industrial transformation, as well as on income distribution, especially the employment of the poor population in Shenzhen, and the effect on poverty reduction of Shenzhen in the region and even the country.

This paper mainly includes four parts: The first part is the discussion as to the effect of the introduction of FDI on local income distribution and poverty reduction; the second part is the investigation of the labor stage and FDI industry character-istics; the third part makes an empirical analysis of the relationship between FDI and employment of the poverty-stricken labor force; and the last part comes to the conclusions and policy implications.

1   Review of the Literature

At present, there are obviously three kinds of controversial views concerning the effect of FDI on the income distribution, employment and income of the poor pop-ulation.

1.1   View 1: The Widening Effect of the Income Distribution Gap

By means of a theoretical analysis and various empirical studies, this kind of view argues that the introduction of FDI worsens the local income distribution and increases the gap between the rich and the poor in the local area, which is not con-ducive to local poverty reduction. The main points come from the research of the following economists:

Mundell (1957), by the teleological analysis of FDI, believed that FDI would first flow into import substitution sectors where the host country did not have comparative advantages. Generally, capital- and technology-intensive industries in developing countries lacked comparative advantages. Therefore, the entry of FDI into these industries would increase wage differentials between skilled and unskilled workers, and have an adverse income distribution effect on the poor people who are mainly non-skilled workers. The empirical analyses of Belderbos and Sleuwagen (1996) and Blondijen (2005) validated this hypothesis. Hossein and John (2002) found that if transnational companies invested in capital- and technology-intensive industries in the host country, this could increase the unemployment rate of non-skilled workers in the host country and widen the income gap.

Feenstra and Hanson (1997) proposed the theory of outsourcing, using data from Mexico to prove that growth in FDI could account for over 50% of the increase in the skilled labor wage share. The study found that FDI deteriorated Mexico's income distribution.

Choi (2004) selected the panel data of 119 countries from 1993 to 2002 to build a regression model of income distribution and FDI. The results showed that the increase of FDI could increase the Gini coefficient, and the FDI outflow had greater influence on the income imbalance than that of FDI inflow.

The research of Chinese scholars mainly focuses on the analysis of domestic cities or regions. Sun (1998) analyzed the effect of FDI on China's regional economic growth and found that FDI was an important factor affecting the income gap between the eastern and western regions of China since the reform and opening-up.

The analysis of Fan and Duan (2003) showed that foreign direct investment has a significant correlation with the income distribution of Chinese residents. With the spillover effect, capital attraction and trade of the industrial chain and foreign-funded sectors, it influences the income gap between foreign-funded and non-foreign-funded sectors, foreign-investment active and scarce regions, thus resulting in an interregional income gap, especially between the eastern and western regions, as well as a nationwide income gap.

Xiaoxia (2008) applied the quarterly time series data during the all-around opening-up period to analyze the effects of foreign trade and FDI on the income and differentiation of farmers in China. The empirical study showed that FDI could lead to an increase in the income of farmers and a decrease in the degree of differentiation. FDI worsened the local income distribution and thus was not conducive to poverty reduction.

1.2   View 2: A Narrowing Effect of Income Distribution Gap

Economists holding this kind of view proved through various theoretical analyses and practices that the introduction of FDI tended to narrow the income gap within the region, improve the income distribution, and help reduce regional poverty. The main research includes:

Kojima et al. (1973) proposed that FDI and trade were complementary. FDI aimed at allocating resources and pursuing cost minimization on a global scale. Therefore, FDI mainly flowed into labor-intensive export sectors with comparative advantages in developing countries, thus promoting the export trade of the host country. In this case, FDI could increase the demand for unskilled workers and increase their wages, reduce the wage differential between skilled and unskilled workers, and have a favorable income distribution effect on the poor population.

Bornal (2004) utilized the US Panel data from 1982 to 1997 to analyze the influencing factors of income inequality (represented by the Gini coefficient) in various states, such as macroscopic, policy and demographic features. The results indicated that except the northeastern United States, FDI inflows significantly decreased the income inequality in other regions.

Jian-hua (2007) employed the 1998–2005 household survey data to empirically study the relationship between FDI and urban poverty in China with the cointegration theory and the vector autoregressive model (VAR). The results revealed that FDI significantly increased the income share of the poor in the total population and therefore it could achieve economic growth beneficial for the poor and a positive poverty reduction effect. However, FDI also aggravated the income inequality within the poor population because the poorer the population was, the less they could benefit from FDI.

Zhang and Zhou (2009), based on the panel data of 30 provinces in China from 1989 to 2006, utilized the GMM method to analyze the direct and indirect effects of FDI on the income inequality in urban and rural areas of China. The results showed that for every 1% increase in FDI, the income gap between urban and rural areas in China was reduced by 0.24%.

1.3 View 3: An Uncertain Effect on the Income Distribution Gap

This kind of view argues that: FDI has an insignificant or an unclear effect on income distribution. There are many ways for FDI to influence local income distribution. The effect depends on the developmental stage of the local economy, the market environment, and the purpose, type, quality and developmental stage of FDI. The main research is:

Agenor (2004) proposed that FDI had nonlinearities and "threshold effects" on the income distribution and poverty. Compared with domestic firms, foreign firms usually adopted more advanced technologies, hired more skilled workers and paid higher efficiency wages, thereby resulting in a widening of the wage gap between skilled and unskilled labor. The widening in wage differentials may lead to investment in human capital and a gradual increase in the supply of skilled labor; this would tend to narrow the wage differential. According to this hypothesis, the relative wage effect of FDI would take the form of an "inverted U-shaped curve" for the relationship between FDI and income gap and poverty. In other words, FDI would benefit the poor only when it reached a certain level. Using panel data from 16 developing countries, including Brazil and Thailand, he found nonlinearities between FDI and poverty. The testing results of Figini and Gorg (2006) also drew the same conclusion.

In the opinion of Aisbett et al. (2005): whether the poor people could benefit from FDI also depended on a range of complementary policies, such as state investment in education and human capital, infrastructure improvements, and credit and technical aid of low-income groups and macroeconomic stability.

Wang (2005) conducted an econometric research on the relationship between FDI and nationwide employment from 1994 to 2002. He pointed out that FDI directly led to a large amount of domestic employment, but indirectly squeezed out the employment by squeezing domestic investment and increasing productivity. His calculations suggested that every 1% of increase in FDI would cause direct employment to rise by 0.052%; also, it would squeeze out 0.049% of domestic investment, which indirectly led to 0.031% of unemployment; and, it could push the productivity level up by 0.146% and indirectly reduce domestic employment opportunities by 0.013%. From 1994 to 2002, the total number of employments directly driven by FDI reached 25.5888 million; the employment loss caused by the crowding out effect totaled 14.8965 million; and the employment loss caused by the increase in productivity brought by FDI totaled 6.6239 million. The total effect of FDI on domestic employment was still positive. Every 1% of increase in FDI could increase real employment by 0.008%. The cumulative total employment caused by FDI increased by 4.0718 million from 1994 to 2002, which contributed greatly to alleviating domestic employment pressure.

2 The Labor Factor and FDI Industrial Stage Characteristics

2.1 Labor Factor Characteristics of the Poor Population

First, these are mainly members of the non-household-registered population characterized by mobility. At the beginning of the establishment of the Shenzhen Special Economic Zone (SEZ), the population was only 332,900, who were mainly members of the household-registered agricultural population, and the non-registered population was only 12,000. After the establishment of the Shenzhen SEZ, the massive influx of migrants caused an explosive population growth in Shenzhen. As of the Sixth National Population Census in 2010, the resident population of Shenzhen reached 10.358 million. The rapidly growing migrant population from all parts of the country, mainly in the economically backward neighboring provinces such as Jiangxi, Hunan, Hubei, Sichuan, Guizhou, and Guangxi, comes primarily for the purposes of finding a job or doing business. Most of these migrants cannot enjoy the household registration of Shenzhen, but these people have worked and lived in Shenzhen for a long period of time and have formed a major part of the Shenzhen population. The non-resident population does not have fixed assets such as land and real estate in Shenzhen. They suffer from hukou (which means "household registration") discrimination and are unable to enjoy the welfare of SEZ households. Their social network in Shenzhen is fragile, they lack credit support, technical assistance, education and training. They cannot enjoy the transfer payments of the state, thus

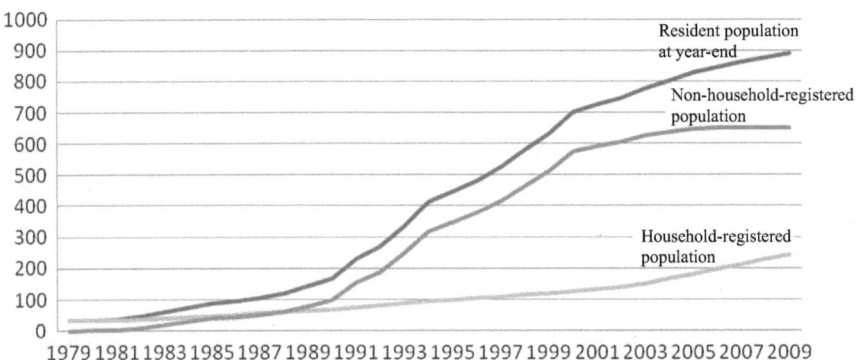

Fig. 1 Household structure changes of the population in Shenzhen. *Data source Statistical Yearbook of Shenzhen* over the years

having greater vulnerability to poverty and being the main poverty-stricken group in Shenzhen (Fig. 1).

Second, the poor population, generally with a low level of education, is highly dependent on the development of labor-intensive industries. At the beginning of the establishment of the SEZ, Shenzhen was dominated by labor-intensive industries and low-skilled workers accounted for the majority. The per capita education period was less than 9 years, and most workers had received junior high school and lower level education. In 1990, up to 76.4% of the workers in Shenzhen had only a junior high school or lower level education. This proportion diminished to 68.4% in 2000; but until 2010, they still accounted for 59% of resident population in the city, including 4,562,700 people with an educational level of junior high school, 92,000 with a level of primary school and 50,200 illiterates. These low-education-level workers mainly work in labor-intensive industries, with low incomes and high unemployment risks, thus making up the majority of the poor population (Table 1).

Third, among the poor population, the proportions of women and young people are high. Among the population of Shenzhen, the rate of participation of women's

Table 1 Distribution of education level per 100,000 inhabitants of Shenzhen

Year	College or higher	Senior high school	Junior high school	Primary school	Proportion below junior high school (%)
1990	4416	19,219	43,534	21,549	76.4
1995	7046	20,856	40,445	19,789	72.1
2000	8381	23,291	54,259	12,563	68.4
2005	13,331	24,547	48,836	11,953	62.1
2010	17,175	23,965	44,050	8883	58.9

Data source Statistical Yearbook of Shenzhen
Unit 10,000 people

labor maintains a fairly high proportion, and such a structure is of great significance for a region's poverty reduction effect. Women who can earn income by entering the labor market and finding jobs are able to play a very significant role in promoting poverty reduction in the region. However, in general, women workers are vulnerable to discrimination on the labor market. The average educational level of the women's labor force is often lower than that of men, so they are at a disadvantage in competition with a higher incidence of poverty. The labor force in Shenzhen is young due to young people, the mobility of the population and developmental characteristics of labor-intensive industries in Shenzhen initially. The young labor force is generally low-skilled labor from poverty-stricken regions with a low level of education. Moreover, young people have fewer savings, no capital income and a greater risk of poverty (Table 2).

2.2 FDI Industrial Stage Characteristics

The developmental stages of FDI and the corresponding FDI industry distribution have different effects on income distribution and poverty reduction in a region. This paper analyzes the evolution of FDI industrial structure in Shenzhen from the perspective of capital source, industrial distribution and capital intensity.

Stage One: from 1979 to the mid-1980s, entry of FDI. At this stage, the cumulative FDI was 5.48 million US dollars, and the investment in "three imports and compensation trade" (which means "processing of imported materials or according to supplied samples, assembling of supplied parts, and compensation trade") was 9.89 million US dollars. The source of funds was mainly Hong Kong and Macao. The foreign investment was concentrated in the fields of industry, commerce, hotel and catering, real estate and transportation. The proportion of investment in fixed assets in sectors such as industry, transportation and real estate was relatively large. This period belonged to the trial stage of opening-up to the outside world. There were few foreign investment projects in small sizes. The actual amount of foreign investment used was very limited (Table 3).

Among the FDI funds introduced in the early stage, the main form of processing trade was the simple "three imports and compensation trade". This meant that foreign investors provided the equipment (including the construction of factories by foreign investors), raw materials and samples, and were responsible for the exportation of all products, and Chinese enterprises contributed the land, the plant and labor. This cooperative production mode had a lower demand for technology. The main industrial products in this stage included: electronic industrial products such as tape recorders, electronic computers, televisions, and daily necessities such as printing and dyeing cloth, apparel, plastics, fertilizers, etc. The mode of production was mainly processing and assembling with a low technical content and a high demand for a labor force.

Stage Two: from the mid-1980s to the mid-1990s, full development of FDI. From 1986 to 1995, investments from Hong Kong and Macao continued to expand, with 10,832 projects, accounting for 86.7% of the agreed foreign investments. At the same

Table 2 Distribution of age group and education level of inhabitants in Shenzhen

	15–19	20–24	25–29	30–34	35–39	40–44	45–49	50–54	55–59
Total	318,156	438,387	220,592	125,618	95,125	62,018	40,453	36,411	28,679
University or higher	1172	6034	8588	3280	2007	2347	4327	4319	1347
Three-year college	1619	8435	9741	5685	4968	3411	2293	2141	1142
Specialized secondary school	4551	8448	8381	4540	3444	3772	2972	2525	993
Senior high school	38,347	92,612	72,166	39,640	18,165	8022	4505	2841	1858
Junior high school	215,303	265,433	96,082	48,228	37,808	21,235	10,853	7388	5169
Primary school	55,720	55,058	23,434	21,258	25,488	20,562	12,264	11,505	9470

Data source The report of the 4th census
Unit people

Table 3 FDI industry distribution in Shenzhen from 1979 to 1985

Sectors	Agriculture	Industry	Transportation	Commerce, hotel and catering	Real estate
Number of projects	69	2159	51	333	120
Amount (USD 10,000)	815	30,650	3081	11,331	25,957
Average amount per project (USD 10,000)	11.8	14.2	60.4	34	216.3

Data source Statistical Yearbook of Shenzhen

time, foreign investments from other countries and regions also developed rapidly. In Asia, the investments increased fastest from Taiwan, Japan, and Singapore, followed by Thailand, South Korea, and Malaysia; and enterprises from developed countries represented by the United States of America and including Britain, Canada, Australia and France also entered Shenzhen. The investment method was mainly joint venture, and the "three imports and compensation trade" was gradually reduced. The form of investment by Sino-foreign joint ventures became dominant, and the wholly foreign-owned enterprises also witnessed a relatively obvious growth.

The investments were gradually expanding into multiple industries. Compared with the first five years of the 1980s, FDI projects in the industry sector increased by 5.1 times, the amount increased by 17.4 times to 5.34 billion US dollars, and in the actual FDI amount, the investment in industry accounted for 62.7%; the real estate industry was the second largest investment sector, the projects grew by 4.4 times, and the amount increased by 3.9 times to a total of 306 million US dollars; the agreed projects in the transportation sector increased by 1.6 times, and the total amount increased to 660 million US dollars; but FDI projects in the agriculture sector fell from 69 in the first stage to 58, the average project amount increased, and the overall scale was still small.

An important change of FDI from 1985 to 1995 was that it entered the sectors of finance and insurance, scientific research and integrated technology services, health care, social security and social welfare, education, culture, sports and entertainment. Among them, the scientific research and integrated technology services found the fastest growth of agreed projects, with a total of 96 signed projects. The finance and insurance sector had the most obvious increase in the actual amount of investment, up to 835 million US dollars. In this stage, FDI also played an important role in the field of infrastructure construction in Shenzhen, such as tunnels, expressways, power plants, and terminals (Table 4).

Meanwhile, there was an industrial adjustment and expansion within the industry sector. In 1986, among industrial enterprises above the designated size in Shenzhen, the labor productivity of FDI enterprises was 85,715 (yuan/person), while the average labor productivity of domestic enterprises was only 26,155 (yuan/person), so the

Table 4 FDI industry distribution in Shenzhen from 1986 to 1995

Sectors	Construction	Health care, social security and social welfare	Education, culture, sports and entertain-ment	Scientific research and integrated technology services	Finance and insurance
Number of projects	62	32	25	85	22
Amount (USD 10,000)	544	11,870	2229	152	74,119
Average amount per project (USD 10,000)	8.8	370.9	89.2	1.8	3369.0

Data source Statistical Yearbook of Shenzhen

labor productivity of FDI enterprises was 3.2 times that of Shenzhen, which dropped to 2.8 times in 1990; in 1995, the average labor productivity of industrial enterprises above the designated size rose to 49,980 (yuan/person), that of Hong Kong, Macao and Taiwan-funded enterprises was only 1.1 times, and that of other foreign-invested enterprises was 100,430 (yuan/person), more than 2 times the average. The emergence of this trend stemmed from the development of local enterprises in Shenzhen and the technology spillover effects of FDI enterprises. During this period, the industrial capital intensity was relatively low. From 1987 to 1995, as calculated at the constant price in 1986, the number of members of the labor force employed by FDI enterprises per 10,000 yuan was 1.22, and the capital owned per FDI employee was 9400 yuan.

Stage Three: after the mid-1990s. After the mid-1990s, Shenzhen began industrial upgrading. The remarkable feature was that the average growth rate of FDIs from Asian countries in Shenzhen slowed down year-on-year, while the proportion of developed countries accelerated significantly. Hong Kong and Macao capitals were still the most important source of FDI in Shenzhen, but with a declining proportion. From 1997 to 2009, the number of Hong Kong and Macao FDI projects totaled 23,974, accounting for 77.2% of foreign investment projects in Shenzhen, but 9.5% points less than the Stage Two. Among Asian countries and regions, South Korea had the most obvious growth, and other countries had relatively stable growth rates. Among Western developed countries, the amount of FDI from Australia and Canada dropped obviously, but that from other countries increased significantly. In general, the scale of unit FDI projects of developed countries was generally higher than that of developing countries, and the form of FDI was mainly the sole proprietorship.

After the mid-1990s, the distribution of FDI sectors began to expand to service and technology-intensive industries. The growth of commerce, scientific research and integrated technology services, transportation, and real estate was the most significant. FDI began to shift to capital- and technology-intensive industries. From the perspective of actual amount of investments, in scientific research and integrated technology services, construction and commerce sectors, the investment growth was the most obvious. Industry was still the main invested sector of FDI, but with the industrial upgrading of the city, the actual FDI per industrial project increased from US$487,000 in the Stage Two to US$1.77 million, and the average investment scale was 3.6 times that of Stage Two. In addition, the scale of individual agreed FDI projects in sectors of construction, scientific research and integrated technology services, health care and social security also increased significantly. The scale of FDI investment was enlarged, and the capital density of FDI investments continued to expand (Table 5).

When the entry period of FDI passes by, the number of the members of the labor force employed per unit FDI began to show a trend from downward to upward development: in Stage Two, from 1987 to 1995, the number of the members of the labor force employed per 10,000 yuan of FDI calculated at the price of 1986 was 1.22 on average, and the amount of capital owned per FDI worker was 9400 yuan (calculated at the constant price of 1986); and in Stage Three, the number of the members of the labor force employed per 10,000 yuan of FDI dropped significantly, and from 1996 to 2003, the number of the members of the labor force employed per 10,000 yuan of FDI calculated at the price of 1986 reduced to 0.71. Similarly, the amount of capital owned per FDI worker showed an increasing trend: an increase to 14,600 yuan. Since 2004, due to the expansion of FDI in the modern service sector, the labor absorption capacity of FDI funds once again showed a significant upward trend. The number of the members of the labor force employed per unit FDI increased greatly. From 2004 to 2009, the number of the members of the labor force employed per 10,000 yuan of FDI calculated at the price of 1986 increased to 1.31, but the average amount of capital owned per FDI worker reduced to 7700 yuan (Fig. 2).

In terms of labor productivity, FDI in this stage was clearly divided into two different levels: the labor productivity of FDI from developed countries represented by the United States of America remained high and it was higher than the average level of Shenzhen from the 1990s to the beginning of the 21st century, but it has declined slightly in recent years; and Hong Kong, Macao and Taiwan-funded enterprises have begun to lag behind the average level since the late 1990s, and the gap has been getting bigger and bigger. The main reasons for this phenomenon included: First, the growth of local enterprises in Shenzhen; second, local enterprises, especially state-owned enterprises, had advantages due to their monopoly of resources; and third, Hong Kong, Macao and Taiwan-funded enterprises failed to complete the transformation in a timely and successful manner (Fig. 3).

Table 5 FDI industry distribution in Shenzhen from 1996 to 2009

Sectors	Agriculture	Industry	Construction	Transportation	Commerce, hotel and catering	Real estate	Health care, social security and social welfare	Education, culture, sports and entertainment	Scientific research and integrated technology services	Finance and insurance
Number of projects (II)	58	10,953	62	80	480	528	32	25	85	22
Number of projects (III)	43	16,610	63	550	6050	2369	15	39	3654	33
Project growth rate	0.7	1.5	1.0	6.9	12.6	4.5	0.5	1.6	43.0	1.5
Amount (II) (USD 10,000)	2332	533,540	544	59,079	18,775	100,595	11,870	2229	152	74,119
Amount (III) (USD 10,000)	3723	2,946,867	42,036	279,584	391,647	471,376	13,599	6568	147,940	118,035
Amount of growth rate	1.6	5.5	77.3	4.7	20.9	4.7	1.1	2.9	973.3	1.6

(continued)

Table 5 (continued)

Sectors	Agriculture	Industry	Construction	Transportation	Commerce, hotel and catering	Real estate	Health care, social security and social welfare	Education, culture, sports and entertainment	Scientific research and integrated technology services	Finance and insurance
Average amount per project (II) (USD 10,000)	40.2	48.7	8.8	738.5	39.1	190.5	370.9	89.2	1.8	3369.0
Average amount per project (III) (USD 10,000)	86.0	177.4	667.2	508.3	64.7	199.0	906.6	168.4	40.5	3576.8
Average growth rate	2.2	3.6	76.0	0.7	1.7	1.0	2.4	1.9	22.6	1.1

Data source Statistical Yearbook of Shenzhen

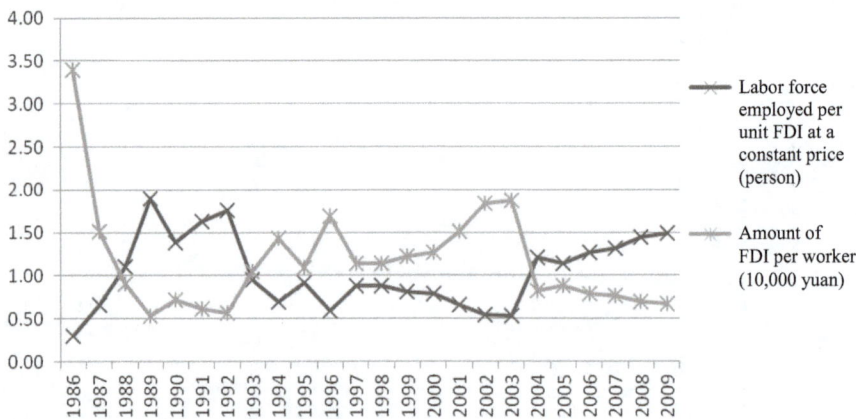

Fig. 2 Capital intensity of FDI funds in Shenzhen (calculated at the constant price of 1986). *Data source Statistical Yearbook of Shenzhen* over the years

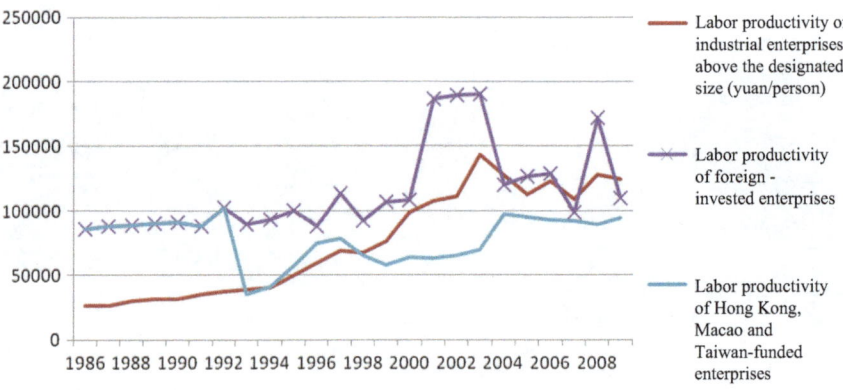

Fig. 3 Comparison of labor productivity of industrial enterprises above the designated size: average, foreign-invested enterprises and Hong Kong, Macao and Taiwan-funded enterprises. *Data source Statistical Yearbook of Shenzhen* over the years

3 Empirical Analysis of the Employment Relationship Between FDI and Poor Workers

3.1 Data Source and Variable Selection

This paper takes the annual data of Shenzhen from 1979 to 2009. The data sources are *Statistical Yearbook of Shenzhen* and the census data of Shenzhen. The variables in the econometric model are processed as follows:

$$LNL = -5.716041903 + 0.9031568594 * LNFDI$$
$$+ [AR(1) = 0.3901075628]$$

First of all, in order to obtain the data for the reasonable poverty reduction effect, this paper has made three necessary and realistic hypotheses: First, the level of education determines the skill level, and the workers with a junior high school and lower level of education are low-skilled workers; second, the skill level determines the level of income, low-skilled workers are low-income workers and belong to the poor population; third, the employment of the poor population means poverty alleviation, and their employment leads to the reduction of poverty in Shenzhen. Therefore, this paper uses the number of employments of low-skilled workers as an explained variable, indicating the number of poverty-reduction people since the establishment of the Shenzhen Special Economic Zone.

Given that there are only a few years of statistical data in Shenzhen, this paper mainly selects two explanatory variables: the actual amount of foreign investment used and the real GDP per capita of Shenzhen. The actual amount of foreign investment used is applied to explain the effect of FDI on the employment of poor workers in Shenzhen, that is, its poverty reduction effect; and the real GDP per capita of Shenzhen is mainly to explain the effects of other major factors on the employment of poor workers. All price data in the model has been converted to RMB prices at the constant price of 1979. At the same time, in order to eliminate the heteroscedasticity of the non-stationary time series and reflect the elastic coefficient between the variables, we logarithmically treat all the data.

3.2 Econometric Analysis

First, simple linear regression is used to estimate the effect of FDI on the employment of poor workers. FDI promotes employment for the poor by directly hiring local labor, creating jobs, promoting employment, or through other indirect employment effects. To find out the relationship between FDI and the employment of low-skilled workers, we use the least squares method to make a simple regression. The regression results are as follows:

$$D(LNL) = 0.7955819835 - 0.05451771968 * LNFDI$$
$$- 0.4700497529 * D(LNRGDP)$$

The regression results show that the random error term has autocorrelation. After using the generalized difference method, the regression results are significant. The various tests are passed, and the goodness of fit is 0.94. The degree of explanation is good. The regression results indicate that there is a significant correlation between employment of low-skilled workers and amount of FDI. For every 1% increase in FDI, the employment of poor workers increases by 0.9% (Fig. 4).

Fig. 4 Unary regression
results of the logarithm
relationship of the actual
amount of foreign investment
used by Shenzhen and the
employment of low-skilled
labor

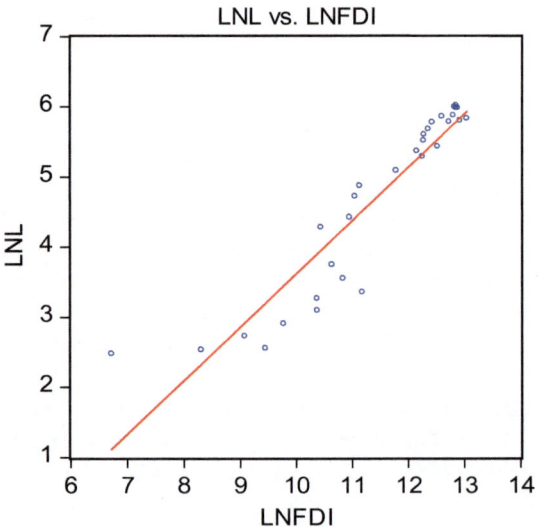

Second, multiple linear regression is applied to analyze the relationship between
FDI and the rate of change of employment of the poor population. We add the
logarithm of Shenzhen's per capita GDP to the original explanatory variable as
LNRGDP. The explained variable is still the logarithm LNL of the employment of the
poor population in Shenzhen. In order to avoid the problem of spurious regression, we
first carried out a stationary test on the data, and LNFDI and LNRGDP stabilize after
lagging behind one period. After the stationary processing, the model is regressed
and the regression results are as follows:

After the stationary processing, the various tests are passed. Since the equation
may miss some important explanatory variables, the goodness of fit is generally 0.45,
but the regression results of the variables are significant. The regression results show
that: if FDI rises by 1%, the growth rate of the employment of the poor population
drops by 0.055% points. For every 1% point of increase in the GDP growth rate, the
growth rate of the employment of the poor population falls by 0.47% points.

The regression results indicate that there is a significant positive correlation
between the employment of low-skilled workers in Shenzhen and the amount of
FDI. For every 1% increase in FDI, the employment of poor workers increases by
0.9%. However, with the growth of FDI, the unit FDI has a negative effect on the
increase in the employment of the members of the labor force. If FDI rises by 1%,
the growth rate of the employment of the poor population falls by 0.055% points.
Combined with the above analysis, it shows that with the industrial upgrading of
Shenzhen and the transformation and development of FDI, the adsorption capacity of FDI in Shenzhen for the employment of low-skilled workers will gradually
decrease, and the direct poverty reduction effect of FDI will gradually weaken.

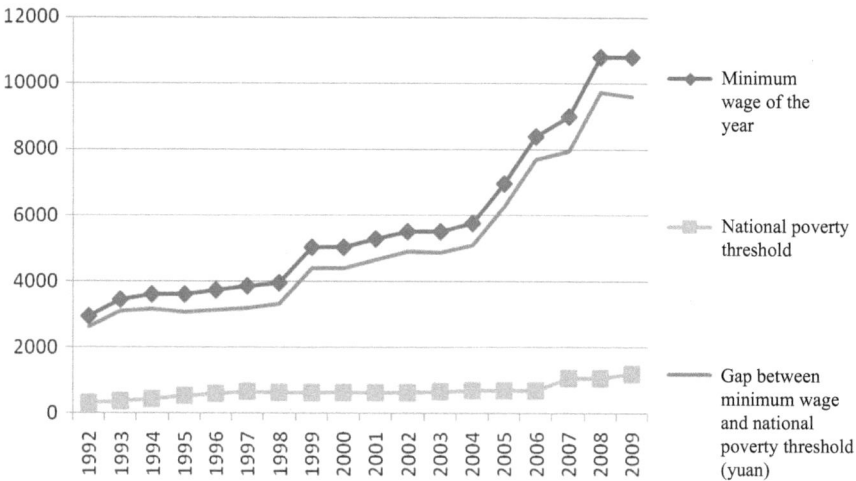

Fig. 5 Comparison of minimum wage of Shenzhen and the national poverty threshold. *Data source Poverty Monitoring Report, Statistical Yearbook of Shenzhen*

3.3 Analysis of the Results

The econometric analysis investigates the employment for low-skilled workers through direct or indirect effects of FDI in Shenzhen, thereby directly helping the workers out of poverty. Since the poor in Shenzhen are mainly workers from poor areas across the country, we are considering those coming from poor families. While the poor workers in Shenzhen themselves are out of poverty, they may use the residual wage after deducting living costs to support their families, thus indirectly helping the families out of poverty. Since the wage level in Shenzhen has been higher than the domestic average for a long time, the indirect effect of wages on the poor after employment cannot be ignored (Fig. 5).

We further hypothesize that the income from wages earned by the poor and their living expenses in Shenzhen are both the ratios of the minimum wage, and the annual residual wage can be obtained from one subtracting another. The indirect poverty reduction effect on the employment of the poor in Shenzhen can be obtained by comparing the national minimum wage with the annual residual wage. As can be seen from the figure below, with the increase in wages of low-skilled workers, the absolute amount of residual wage earned by the poor workers in Shenzhen has grown rapidly from 222 yuan in 1979 to 4860 yuan in 2009. If the officially announced poverty threshold is used as the criterion, the poverty reduction effects become more and more effective for the poverty-stricken workers in Shenzhen. The number of people who have been lifted out of poverty has risen from two in the early 1980s to four to five in the new century. There are three reasons: First, due to the rapid growth of wages in Shenzhen, the wage income of poor workers has also increased significantly; second, the residual wage of poor workers may be overestimated because the living expenses

Table 6 Residual wage and poverty reduction capability of poverty-stricken workers in Shenzhen

Year	Number of low-skilled laborers (10,000 people)	Average annual wage of low-skilled laborers (yuan)	Cost of living of low-income people in Shenzhen (yuan)	Annual residual wage (yuan)	Poverty threshold of China (yuan)	Ratio of residual wage and poverty threshold of China	Possible poverty-alleviated population (10,000 people)
1980	12.6	769	492	277	120	2	25.2
1985	26.25	1721	1101	620	206	3	78.75
1990	83.41	2775	1776	999	300	3	250.23
1995	215.22	4500	2880	1620	530	3	645.66
2000	324.54	6285	4022	2263	625	4	1298.16
2005	357.98	8700	5568	3132	683	5	1789.9
2009	412.02	13,500	8640	4860	1196	4	1648.08

Data source Estimated according to the *Statistical Yearbook of Shenzhen*

of the poor in Shenzhen may be underestimated; third, the poverty threshold officially announced by the government is too low and remains at the level of meeting basic calories and solving food and clothing problems, thus seriously underestimating the living costs of the poor. With the development of China's economy, the living standards of the localities where the poor people living in Shenzhen come from have exceeded the national poverty threshold, so the actual poverty reduction effect of the employment of poor people in Shenzhen is seriously overestimated. If we take full account of the rising cost of living in Shenzhen and the relative improvement of the living standards of the poor in the country, the poverty reduction effect of employment of poverty-stricken workers in Shenzhen will be significantly weakened (Table 6).

4 Conclusions and Suggestions

This paper studies the characteristics of the labor factor of the poor population and the characteristics of the industrial structure of FDI in Shenzhen, and profoundly discusses the relationship between the FDI in Shenzhen and the employment of poor workers. The main conclusions are:

(1) The development of FDI in Shenzhen is characterized by stages, which are reflected in the stages of FDI sector distribution changing from industry, commerce, hotel and catering, and real estate towards finance and insurance, scientific research and integrated technology services, and expanding to the technology-intensive sectors. The level of technology, labor productivity, and labor adsorption capacity of capital show a staged trend. In the early stages of development, the labor productivity of FDI funds is significantly higher than

the average level of domestic enterprises above the designated size. With the growth of local Chinese enterprises, the labor productivity of FDI enterprises begins to be equal; the labor productivity of FDI enterprises from developed countries is higher than the average domestic level, but the gap has a significant trend towards narrowing; and the labor productivity of FDI enterprises from Hong Kong and Macao becomes significantly lower than the average level of domestic enterprises above the designated size. The labor adsorption capacity of FDI sectors has several stages of development: from 1987 to 1995, the average number of members of the labor force employed per 10,000 yuan of FDI was 1.22; after 1996, that number was significantly reduced, even to 0.71 from 1996 to 2003; after 2004, due to the service trend of the industrial structure, the labor adsorption capacity of FDI once again showed a significant upward trend, and from 2004 to 2009, the number of members of the labor force employed per 10,000 yuan of FDI increased to 1.31.

(2) There is a significant positive correlation between FDI and employment of low-skilled workers in Shenzhen. For every 1% of increase in the amount of FDI funds, the employment of low-skilled workers increases by 0.9%. FDI affects the employment of low-skilled workers through the transfer mechanisms such as direct employment effects, indirect employment effects and human capital effects, and thus helps reduce poverty. The experience of Shenzhen proves that the growth of FDI funds is conducive to the employment of the poor and has positive effects on poverty reduction.

(3) The effect of FDI on the employment rate of the poor population in Shenzhen has a staged feature. With the evolution of FDI sectors, the growth rate of employment driven by unit FDI has declined: for a 1% increase in FDI, the growth rate of the employment of the poor population drops by 0.055% points. For every 1% point of increase in GDP growth rate, the growth rate of the employment of the poor population falls by 0.47% points.

The implied policy connotation of this paper is: In the initial stage of economic development, the introduction of FDI with poverty reduction as the main goal should be based on the strategy of guiding labor-intensive industrial capital, and the premature pursuit of capital-intensive industries and high-level technology industries is not conducive to the employment of low-income workers, which in turn affects the realization of the goal of poverty reduction.

References

Fan Yanhui, Duan Junshan, Foreign Direct Investment (FDI) and Income Distribution of Chinese Residents [J], *Finance & Economics*, 2003(2).

Feenstra R. C., Hanson G. H. Foreign Direct Investment and Relative wages: Evidence from Mexico's maquiladoras [J]. Journal of International Economics, 1997 (42).

R.A. Mundell. International Trade and Factor Mobility, American Economic Review, 47, 1957, 321–35.

Sun H. Foreign Investment and Economic Development in China [J]. London: ash gate publishing limited, 1998.

Wang Jian, Measuring the Effects of Employment Creation of FDI in China [J], *Statistical Research*, 2005(3).

Zhang Guangsheng, Zhou Juan, Empirical Analysis of the Impact of FDI on China's Urban-rural Income Inequality—Based on GMM Analysis of Inter-provincial Panel Data [J], *Finance & Economics*, 2009(2).

Zhang Quanhong, Zhang Jian-hua, The Impact of FDI on Urban Poverty in China—Co-integration Test Based on Household Survey Data from 1985 to 2005 [J], *Journal of International Trade*, 2007(9).

Zhao Wei, Zhao Xiaoxia, The Roles of Typical Openness Forms to Income and the Income Inequality in Chinese Rural Areas—Based on the Quarterly Data in the Comprehensive Open Period [J], *Journal of International Trade*, 2008(3).

Yuan Yiming Deputy Director of the China Center for Special Economic Zone Research, Shenzhen University, Professor, Ph.D. Supervisor, with research interests in industrial organization and structures.

He Lei Postdoctoral Researcher at the Shenzhen Stock Exchange Research Institute, with research interests in Western economics.

Chapter 2
Theoretical and Empirical Research on the Industrial Restructuring in Shenzhen

Dong Xiaoyuan

Abstract This paper first raises the four "unsustainable" problems of "land, resource, population and environment" faced by Shenzhen. Then, according to optimization and industrial restructuring, after the comprehensive consideration of relevant state policies, academic achievements and data availability, the following five criteria are proposed: production efficiency, profit and tax contribution, resource consumption, environmental friendliness, and industry relevance. In our opinion, the industrial sectors with higher production efficiency, more per capita profit and tax contributions, less resource consumption, less pollution, higher industry relevance and faster technological progress are the sectors with a high degree of quality, and vice versa. Finally, an empirical study is made on the desirable and undesirable changes in the industrial structure of Shenzhen, and the relevant policy suggestions are given.

Keywords Industrial restructuring · Industrial upgrading · Optimization of industrial structure

1 The Problems

Since its establishment, the Shenzhen Special Economic Zone maintains rapid and sustainable economic and social development and has made remarkable achievements, and is thus a miracle of industrialization and urbanization in the world. In recent years, the four "unsustainable" problems of "land, resources, population and environment" faced by Shenzhen are increasingly obvious, and it has become one of the megacities in China that are indeed confronted with the hard constraints of resources and environment.

D. Xiaoyuan (✉)
Institute of Economics, Shenzhen Academy of Social Sciences, Shenzhen 518000, Guangdong, China
e-mail: 6316808@qq.com

© Social Sciences Academic Press 2020

Y. Yuan (ed.), *Studies on China's Special Economic Zones 3*,
Research Series on the Chinese Dream and China's Development Path,
https://doi.org/10.1007/978-981-13-9841-4_2

If Shenzhen can completely transform its developmental model, significantly reduce the speed of development, and focus on improving the efficiency of the utilization of the developed land, there would be no need to worry about the problem of Shenzhen not having any land available in a few years; if Shenzhen can change its economic growth mode and no longer rely on the increasing factor input, but on innovation and technological advancement to achieve economic growth, then the sustained rapid economic growth of Shenzhen will not need any more labor input, and the population pressure on the city will not continue to increase; at the same time, with the technological progress and continuous improvement of the efficiency of production, the energy and water consumption per unit of output will continue to decline, pollution emissions will also decrease, and the pressure of economic growth on resources and environment will be relatively reduced.

Therefore, in order to effectively break the "four unsustainable" bottlenecks, it is necessary to accelerate the transformation of the economic growth mode and speed up the optimization and upgrading of Shenzhen's industrial structure. Specifically, industrial sectors with "high input, high consumption, high pollution and low efficiency" must be restricted and eliminated and those with "low input, low consumption, low pollution and high efficiency" will be supported and encouraged.

2 Theoretical Basis for the Industrial Restructuring in Shenzhen

To optimize the industrial structure of Shenzhen and accelerate industrial upgrading, it is necessary to clearly identify which industrial sectors are to be restricted and eliminated, and which sectors should be encouraged and supported. According to the classification in the *Statistical Yearbook of Shenzhen*, industry can be subdivided into 39 sectors. Which of these sectors should be encouraged and which should be restricted? What are the criteria and basis for policy selection?

Regarding the optimization and adjustment of the industrial structure, considering the relevant state policies, academic achievements and data availability, we propose the following five criteria: production efficiency, profit and tax contributions, resource consumption, environmental friendliness, and industry relevance.

The industrial sectors with higher production efficiency, more per capita profit and tax contributions, less resource consumption, less pollution, higher industry relevance and faster technological progress are the sectors with a high degree of quality, and vice versa. Of course, there are many criteria that can be referenced for choices of industrial optimization, such as productivity growth, growth stamina (revenue elasticity), shortage substitution elasticity, the "bottleneck" effect, industry coordination, currency withdrawal, high added value, marginal savings rate, employment and so on.

2.1   Comparison of Production Efficiency

Production efficiency or labor productivity indicator is of special significance for the industrial restructuring of Shenzhen. Shenzhen needs to maintain a stable economic growth with the control of the total population. Under this constraint, it should either increase the proportion of industrial added value and industrial employees of the sectors with high production efficiency (reducing the proportion of labor-intensive sectors), generally increase the labor productivity of all sectors, or both. There is no other choice.

Industry in Shenzhen consists of more than 30 sectors, including electronics, machinery, textiles, clothing, chemicals, food and medicine. The products in these sectors are diverse, production technology and process are significantly different, and labor productivity varies greatly. From the data of industrial enterprises above the designated size, the sector with the highest labor productivity (petroleum and natural gas extraction) had an annual per capita added value of 24.637 million yuan in 2010, while the sector with the lowest productivity (cultural, educational and sports goods) had an annual per capita added value of only 33,000 yuan, and the difference between them was 736 times. The total labor productivity of Shenzhen's industry is determined by these various sectors with different labor productivities.

Compared by the labor productivity comparison coefficient, it has been found that in 38 industrial sectors with statistical data in the *Statistical Yearbook of Shenzhen* from 1992 to 2011, the labor productivity of the six sectors was lower than the industry average for 20 consecutive years, including electric equipment and machinery, rubber products, plastic products, furniture manufacturing, logging and transportation of timber and bamboo, garments and other fiber products, the mining and dressing of other minerals, and cultural, educational and sports goods; the labor productivity of the six sectors has always been higher than the industry average, including tobacco processing, production and supply of electric power, steam and hot water, medical and pharmaceutical products, production and supply of tap water, beverage manufacturing, electronic and telecommunication equipment, petroleum and natural gas extraction, and food processing; and 22 sectors fluctuate up and down around the average level, including petroleum processing and coking, smelting and pressing of ferrous metals, raw chemical materials and chemical products, smelting and pressing of nonferrous metals, nonmetal mineral products, production and supply of gas, chemical fibers, transportation equipment, special purpose equipment, printing and recording medium reproduction, papermaking and paper products, mining and processing of nonmetal ores, food manufacturing, instruments, meters, cultural and office, ordinary machinery, processing of timber, the manufacture of wood, bamboo, rattan, palm, and straw products, the textile industry, nonferrous metals mining and dressing, recycling and disposal of waste, the manufacturing of metal products, other manufacturing as well as leather, fur, feather and related products.

In terms of sectoral structure, those with a low labor productivity employ most of the labor force. Therefore, to alleviate the population pressure of the development of the secondary industry in Shenzhen, it is important to improve the labor productivity of sectors with a low degree of efficiency of production. A large amount of data shows that in the vertical comparisons of the same sector, labor productivity was higher during the years when the level of per capita capital equipment was higher. Moreover, the horizontal comparisons between different sectors also found that the sectors with a high level of per capita capital equipment were able to achieve higher labor productivity. The level of per capita capital equipment is the primary factor affecting labor productivity. Therefore, the main ways to improve labor productivity are to enhance the level of per capita capital equipment, accelerate technological progress, and optimize industrial structure.

2.2 Comparison of Economic Benefits

1. Per capita profit and tax contribution

Similar to the comparison of labor productivity, although different industrial sectors may have big or small per capita profit and tax contribution in different years, after comparing by means of the comparison coefficient of per capita profit and tax contribution, we found that the sectors with lower labor productivity will have a lower per capita profit and tax contribution; and vice versa.

Because the employee compensation and fixed asset consumption cannot be negative, there is less profit and fewer taxes than the industrial added value. Therefore, in general, industrial sectors with lower per capita added value (labor productivity) have less per capita profit and tax contribution. Among the 38 industrial sectors with statistical data in Shenzhen, the per capita profit and tax contribution of four sectors was higher than the industry average in these 18 years. They are also the sectors with high labor productivity, namely tobacco processing, production and supply of electric power, steam and hot water, medical and pharmaceutical products and beverage manufacturing. Meanwhile, the four sectors with consistently low labor productivity and per capita profit and tax contribution account for a large proportion of the employed population of Shenzhen, but show a downward trend, indicating that the employment structure of industry in Shenzhen has gradually improved, but in the past ten years, this downward trend is not obvious.

2. Profit ratio

We use the "ratio of profit to cost and expenses" indicator in the statistical yearbook to measure economic benefits of various sectors. The industrial sectors with a high ratio of profit to cost and expenses and 10 years of the comparison coefficient of ratio of profit to cost and expenses from 2001 to 2010 being larger than 1 include: petroleum and natural gas extraction, tobacco processing, production and supply of electric power, steam and hot water, beverage manufacturing, printing and recording medium reproduction. The industrial sectors with a low ratio of profit to cost and expenses and 0 year of the comparison coefficient of ratio of profit to cost and expenses from 2001 to 2010 being larger than 1 include: electric equipment and machinery, papermaking and paper products, electronic and telecommunication equipment, instruments, meters, cultural and office equipment, food processing, garments and other fiber products, cultural, educational and sports goods, furniture manufacturing, and the smelting and pressing of ferrous metals. Other sectors have a moderate ratio of profit to cost and expenses and 9 years of the comparison coefficient of ratio of profit to cost and expenses from 2001 to 2010 being larger than 1.

2.3 Comparison of Energy Consumption

According to the data provided in the *Statistical Yearbook of Shenzhen* (2010–2011), sectors with high energy consumption include chemical fibers, production and distribution of electric power and heat power, raw chemical materials and chemical, smelting and pressing of ferrous metals, transportation equipment, the manufacturing of nonferrous metal products, beverage manufacturing and metal products. Those with low energy consumption include the processing of petroleum, coking and processing of nuclear fuel, medical and pharmaceutical products, the manufacture of leather, fur, feather and related products, the manufacture of communication equipment, computers and other electronic equipment, production and distribution of gas, recycling and disposal of waste, and tobacco manufacturing. Other sectors have moderate energy consumption.

2.4 Comparison of Environmental Friendliness

Only by continuous reduction of consumption and pollution can we achieve the goal of sustainable development. The situation of pollution of various sectors is undoubtedly an important basis for industrial optimization. However, the system of statistical indicators in this regard has not yet been established and the relevant information is very difficult to obtain. Here, we can only compare the wastewater discharge and exhaust emissions of various industrial sectors in Shenzhen according to the relevant information provided by the Environmental Protection Bureau in 2005. The comparison coefficient of wastewater discharge ranks from high to low: production and supply of tap water, textile industry, beverage manufacturing, non-metal mineral products, metal products, leather, fur, feather and related products, food manufacturing, food processing, instruments, meters, cultural and office equipment, electronic and telecommunication equipment, as well as electric equipment and machinery. The comparison coefficient of wastewater discharge is 0 for the other sectors. The comparison coefficient of exhaust emissions ranks from high to low: production and supply of electric power, steam and hot water, leather, fur, feather and related products, the textile industry, printing and recording medium reproduction, beverage manufacturing, food manufacturing, nonmetal mineral products, metal products, as well as electronic and telecommunication equipment. The comparison coefficient of exhaust emissions is 0 for the other sectors.

2.5 Comprehensive Evaluation of the Degree of Quality of Industry by Multiple Indicators

Compared with the industry relevance, the degree of environmental friendliness has little value for reference because of outdated and incomplete data. There are only complete statistical data of four indicators: labor productivity, per capita profit and tax contribution, ratio of profit to cost and expenses and energy consumption per unit output. The comprehensive evaluation of the degree of quality of industry is based on these indicators.

Since the energy consumption per unit output is an inverse indicator (the bigger, the worse), we take its comparison coefficient as a negative number, and then directly add (equal weighting) to the comparison coefficients of labor productivity, per capita profit and tax contribution and so on. The comprehensive scores are detailed as follows.

In Table 1, it can be observed that the industrial sectors of Shenzhen can be divided into three categories.

1st Category: High Quality Sectors
These sectors have a comprehensive score of 2 or more on multiple indicators, with high labor productivity, big per capita profit and tax contribution, good profitability and low energy consumption per unit output, and therefore their development should be encouraged. This category includes: petroleum and natural gas extraction, tobacco processing, production and supply of electric power, steam and hot water, production and supply of gas, smelting and pressing of ferrous metals, petroleum processing and coking, production and supply of tap water, medical and pharmaceutical products, food processing, beverage manufacturing and electronic and telecommunication equipment.

2nd Category: Low Quality Sectors
These sectors have a comprehensive score smaller than 0, with low labor productivity, small per capita profit and tax contribution, bad profitability and high energy consumption per unit output, and therefore their development should be restricted. This category includes: chemical fibers, transportation equipment, cultural, educational and sports goods, metal products, raw chemical materials and chemical products, the textile industry, timber processing, bamboo, cane, palm fiber and straw products, plastic products and furniture manufacturing.

3rd Category: General Sectors
These sectors have a comprehensive score higher than 0 and lower than 2.

Table 1 Comprehensive evaluation of the degree of quality of industry

Industries	Mean comparison coefficient of production efficiency (2001–2010)	Mean comparison coefficient of per capita profit and tax contribution (2001–2010)	Mean comparison coefficient of ratio of profit to cost and expenses (2001–2010)	Mean comparison coefficient of energy consumption per unit output (2009–2010)	Comprehensive score
Petroleum and natural gas extraction	483.3	891.8	25.3	1.7	1398.7
Tobacco processing	25.7	66.3	5.2	0.1	97.1
Production and supply of electric power, steam and hot water	22.4	37.6	3	5.2	57.8
Production and supply of gas	14.5	25.4	1.6	0.2	41.3
Smelting and pressing of ferrous metals	3.6	17.3	0.3	3.7	17.5
Petroleum processing and coking	6.9	7.4	1.1	0.4	15.0
Production and supply of tap water	3.3	4.4	2.5	0.7	9.5
Medical and pharmaceutical products	2.4	3	2.2	0.4	7.2
Food processing	2.5	2	0.6	1.0	4.1
Beverage manufacturing	2.2	2.8	1.5	2.5	4.0

(continued)

Table 1 (continued)

Industries	Mean comparison coefficient of production efficiency (2001–2010)	Mean comparison coefficient of per capita profit and tax contribution (2001–2010)	Mean comparison coefficient of ratio of profit to cost and expenses (2001–2010)	Mean comparison coefficient of energy consumption per unit output (2009–2010)	Comprehensive score
Electronic and telecommunication equipment	1.3	1.1	0.6	0.2	2.8
Special purpose equipment	0.7	0.7	1.4	0.9	1.9
Ordinary machinery	0.6	0.7	1.3	1.1	1.5
Printing and recording media reproduction	0.7	0.7	1.3	1.3	1.4
Other manufacturing	0.6	0.5	0.7	0.6	1.2
Leather, fur, feather and related products	0.3	0.3	0.8	0.3	1.1
Instruments, meters, cultural and office equipment	0.7	0.5	0.6	0.7	1.1
Smelting and pressing of nonferrous metals	0.9	0.7	0.6	1.2	1.0
Electric equipment and machinery	0.5	0.4	0.8	0.9	0.8
Nonmetal mineral products	1	0.9	1.3	2.6	0.6
Food manufacturing	0.7	0.6	0.8	1.6	0.5

(continued)

Table 1 (continued)

Industries	Mean comparison coefficient of production efficiency (2001–2010)	Mean comparison coefficient of per capita profit and tax contribution (2001–2010)	Mean comparison coefficient of ratio of profit to cost and expenses (2001–2010)	Mean comparison coefficient of energy consumption per unit output (2009–2010)	Comprehensive score
Papermaking and paper products	0.5	0.4	0.7	1.3	0.3
Rubber products	0.5	0.4	0.9	1.6	0.2
The mining and dressing of other minerals	0	0	0.1		0.1
Garments and other fiber products	0.3	0.1	0.5	0.8	0.1
Furniture manufacturing	0.4	0.2	0.4	1.0	0.0
Plastic products	0.4	0.2	0.6	1.4	−0.2
Timber processing, bamboo, cane, palm fiber and straw products	0.4	0.5	0.7	1.9	−0.3
Textile industry	0.5	0.3	0.7	1.9	−0.4
Raw chemical materials and chemical products	1.2	1.6	1.4	4.7	−0.5
Metal products	0.6	0.5	0.8	2.5	−0.6
Cultural, education and sports goods	0.3	0.1	0.4	1.9	−1.1
Transportation equipment	0.5	0.4	0.6	2.6	−1.1
Chemical fibers	0.9	0.8	1	12.5	−9.8

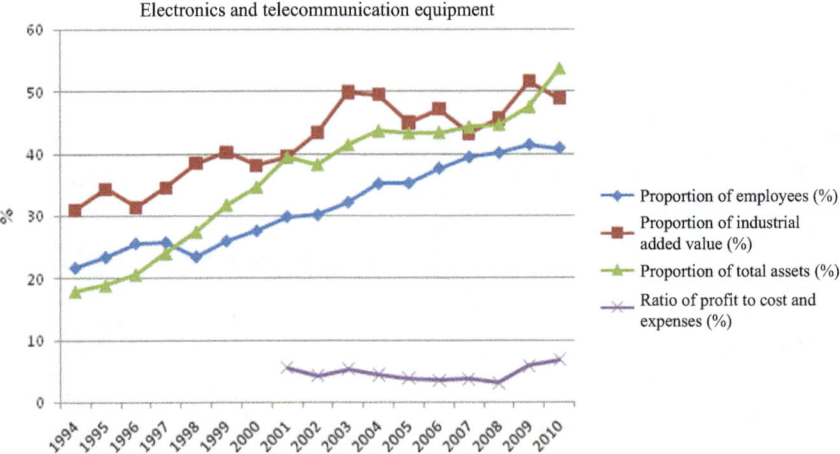

Fig. 1 .

3 Empirical Analysis of Changes in the Industrial Structure of Shenzhen

3.1 Some Changes in the Industrial Structure are Desirable

The desirability of industrial structure changes is first reflected by: the increasing proportion of some high-quality industrial sectors (such as electronics and telecommunication equipment) in the gross industrial output and employment, as shown in Fig. 1.

The desirability of industrial structure changes is also reflected by: the obviously declining trend of some low-quality industrial sectors in gross industrial output and employment, such as chemical fibers, cultural, educational and sports goods, the textile industry, timber processing, bamboo, cane, palm, fiber and straw products, as shown in Fig. 2.

3.2 Some Changes in the Industrial Structure are Undesirable

The undesirability of industrial structure changes is first reflected by: the obviously declining trend of some high-quality industrial sectors in gross industrial output and employment, such as medical and pharmaceutical products, the production and supply of electric power, steam and hot water, tobacco processing, food processing and beverage manufacturing, as shown in Fig. 3.

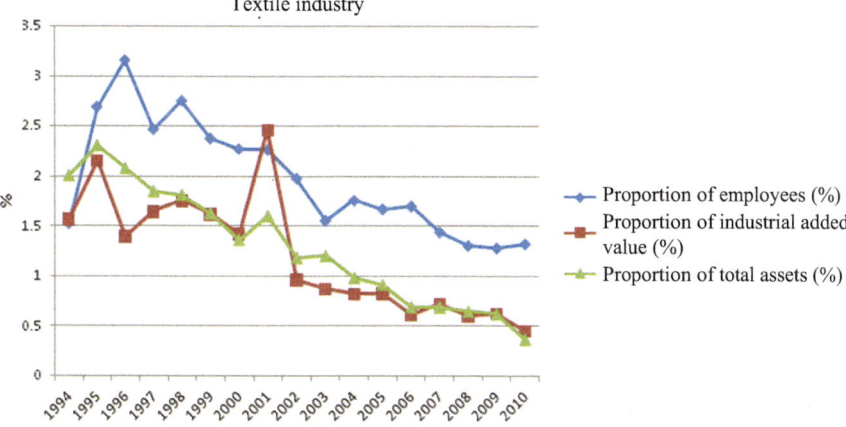

Fig. 2 .

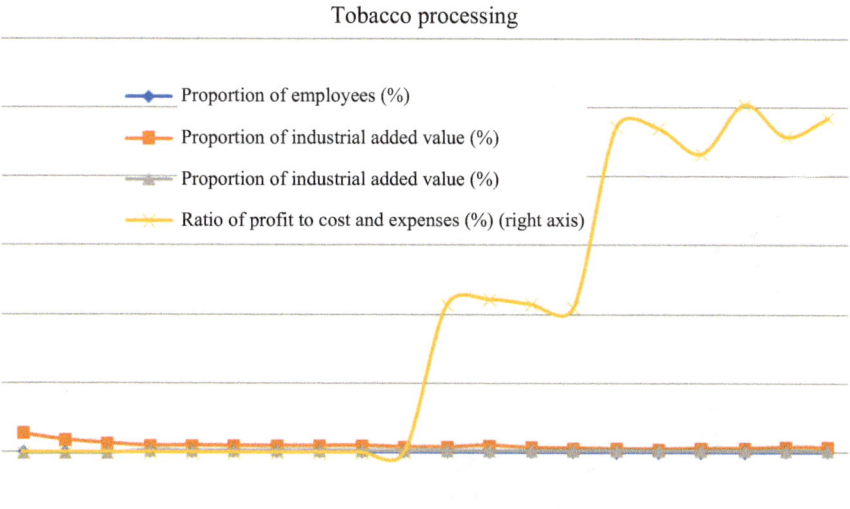

Fig. 3 .

The undesirability of industrial structure changes is also reflected by: no long-term declining trend of some low-quality industrial sectors in gross industrial output and employment, such as furniture manufacturing, as shown in Fig. 4.

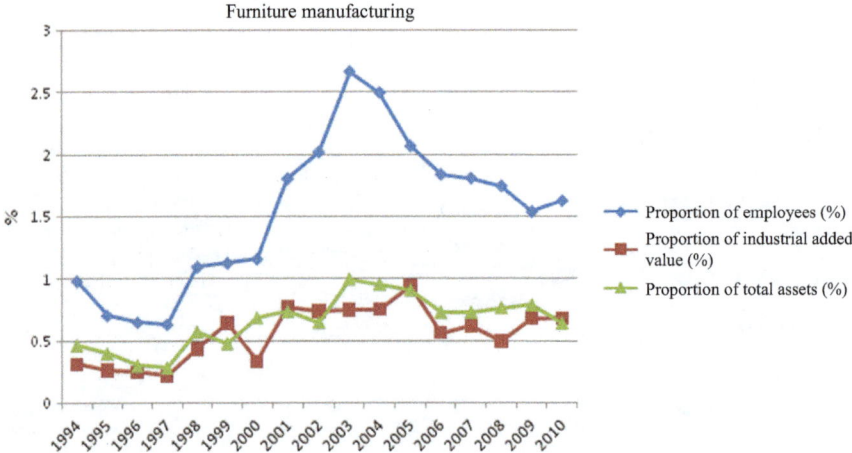

Fig. 4 .

3.3 Whether the Industrial Structure and Its Changes are Reasonable Depends on the Criteria

As stated above, whether the industrial structure is reasonable and whether its evolution is desirable, to a large extent, depends on the criteria for evaluation. Applying different evaluation indicators, the weights of these indicators are different and the conclusions vary accordingly. Although production efficiency, economic benefit and energy consumption are very important, they are not comprehensive enough. The conclusions drawn from them are sometimes too simple or even one-sided. For example, it seems that tobacco processing, with high labor productivity, big per capita profit and tax contribution, good profitability and low energy consumption, should be vigorously developed. However, "smoking is harmful to health" becomes a consensus, the number of smokers is gradually decreasing and the potential for sales growth of tobacco is limited. Therefore, from the perspective of maintaining the balance between supply and demand within the market, it is reasonable to say that the proportion of tobacco processing in industrial output and employment is on the decrease.

According to H. B. Chenery's industrialization stages, the early stage of industrialization is dominated by the food, textile and leather sectors. In the middle stage of industrialization, there are mainly nonmetal minerals, rubber, petrochemical, coal and other sectors. In the late stage of industrialization, metal products, machinery and daily necessities are the mainstream sectors. With the continuous advancement of Shenzhen's industrialization process (some scholars point out that Shenzhen has entered the late stage of industrialization or even post-industrialization[1]), it is

---

[1]See: "Scholars Claimed that Shenzhen Has Entered the Post-Industrial Society", in: *Shenzhen Economic Daily*, 2009-09-05 Column A3. Huang Qunhui, Deputy Director General of Bureau of

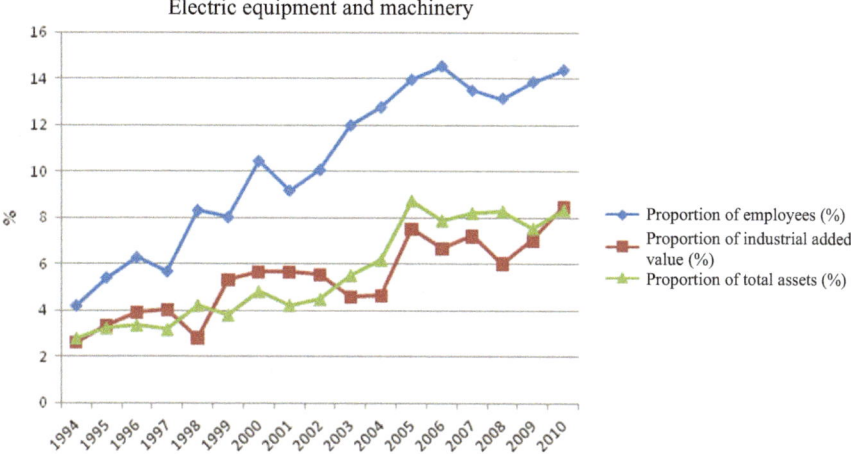

Fig. 5 .

inevitable and reasonable that the proportion of food processing and beverage manufacturing in industrial output and employment of Shenzhen declines.

According to Masayuki Otaki's strategic industry priority growth theory: the three groups of strategic industrial sectors, namely power, machinery and electronics, can effectively exert the effects of industrial relevance and the effects of technology relevance in production, sales and exports, and break the bottleneck of economic development. Based on this criterion, many performances of the industrial structure changes in Shenzhen in the past 20 years are desirable, such as the increasing proportion of electric equipment and machinery, ordinary machinery, special purpose equipment, and electronic and telecommunication equipment in industrial output and employment, as shown in Fig. 5.

3.4 Conclusions and Suggestions

Judging from the theories of industrial structure and the basic requirements of policies, most of the changes in Shenzhen's industrial structure are in line with expectations in the past two decades. The process of industrial upgrading in Shenzhen is basically reasonable.

It should be pointed out that according to the years of practice at home and abroad, technology innovation and technology diffusion are the internal driving forces for industrial upgrading, and there is no fixed model for the optimization of industrial

Scientific Research Management of the China Academy of Social Sciences also pointed out that: "Shanghai and Beijing have already entered into the post-industrial stage, Tianjin and Guangdong are in the second half of the late stage of industrialization…". See: http://szsb.sznews.com/html/2010-03/01/content_976034.htm.

structure. Industrial sectors supported by the government policies alone cannot withstand the pressure of competition on the international and domestic markets. From an international perspective, countries with prevailing industrial policies have already had many problems. For example, large-size enterprises that the government favors have continuous large-scale losses. The government's failure to save them encumbers finance and leads to the outbreak of crisis. This deepens people's doubts about the effectiveness of industrial policies. From the domestic point of view, the government plays a dominant role, chases new concepts, goes all out and advances quickly, and finally results in overcapacity. The Chinese government-guided investment has never run out of such a vicious circle, which applies to iron and steel, chemical and new energy industries. The facts show that there are not many successful cases but a lot of failures in the government's industrial policies. The industrial sectors that the government encourages often cannot develop well, but those without being guided and encouraged can grow strong.

It is clear that the government, like enterprises, does not have complete information on the prospects for economic development; the government and enterprises are both facing the uncertainty of economic operations. Although collecting and mastering more information can reduce uncertainty to a certain extent, this cannot completely eliminate the uncertainty in economic life because the world is not strictly deterministic. In terms of incentives, the government has serious shortcomings compared with enterprises. The development of the industry is related to the government officials' achievements and promotion at most. However, for enterprises, it is a matter of life and death. Therefore, enterprises have more enthusiasm, initiative and depth for searching and researching the market information than the government. Despite owning massive resources, the judgment of the situations of supply and demand and the changing prospects of the industry by the government often does not have the advantages of possessing more information than enterprises. Too many countries adopting the planned economy in the world find mistakes and imbalances over and over again and finally have to change their path and turn to a market economy. This sufficiently demonstrates that the government is unable to truly plan the industrial development in a "planned and proportionate" manner and cannot be more forward-looking and more efficient than the market. Moreover, the more and more detailed the government manages, the more restrictions on the autonomy of enterprises' business operations, and the weaker their ability and willingness to be self-financing. Accordingly, the government should have a full understanding of the limitations of its own capabilities, and should not manage the industrial restructuring too much. If you manage too much, it is easy to return to the old road of a planned economy.

Therefore, the optimization of industrial structure should be the result of "market choice" rather than "government choice". All sectors should have equal opportunities for development. Only those standing out in the fierce market competition are the industrial sectors that are efficient and should be developed. Only by giving all sectors the opportunity to compete fairly, can the industrial structure be well adaptive and flexible towards changes in the international and domestic market demands. The role of government is indeed important, but this role does not mean formulating and implementing industrial policies, but improving the environment for productivity growth (such as improving the quality and efficiency of corporate input factors and infrastructure), developing rules and policies to promote innovation, and keeping and overseeing rules to reduce the transaction costs of the entire society.

Dong Xiaoyuan Director of the Institute of Economics, Shenzhen Academy of Social Sciences, Researcher, Ph.D. of Economics, with research interests in macroeconomics, regional economics, quantitative economics, etc.

Chapter 3
Exploration on Shenzhen's Financial Innovation

Guo Maojia and Long Kai

Abstract Nowadays, various regions and financial institutions in China are launching a new round of financial innovation in order to gain the next round of competitive advantages. As a pioneer of China's reform and opening-up, Shenzhen must naturally consider what principles should be followed in financial innovation, what model should be adopted, what timing should be chosen, what kind of ideas should be implemented, and what content should be included.

Keywords Shenzhen · Financial · Innovation

1 Principles of Shenzhen's Financial Innovation

A consensus seems to have been reached on why Shenzhen should carry out financial innovation and its advantages in financial innovation. However, there are different opinions on the question of what principles should be followed in Shenzhen's financial innovation. In our opinion, to improve the efficiency of Shenzhen's financial innovation, the following four principles must be followed:

1. The principle of serving the real economy. The United States subprime mortgage crisis has warned us that the dazzling financial innovations that are divorced from the objective needs of the real economy are not only unhelpful for the steady growth of the economy and finance, but rather the root cause of the economic and financial bubbles. Therefore, Shenzhen's financial innovation cannot be separated from the development of its real economy. Only in this way will Shenzhen's future financial innovation have a long-lasting vitality.
2. The principle of making steady progress. Because financial innovation is subject to restrictions such as economic system, developmental stage, technical conditions, and the degree of development of financial markets, Shenzhen's financial

G. Maojia (✉) · L. Kai
China Center for Special Economic Zone Research,
Shenzhen University, Shenzhen 518060, Guangdong, China
e-mail: guom123@sina.com

© Social Sciences Academic Press 2020   37
Y. Yuan (ed.), *Studies on China's Special Economic Zones 3*,
Research Series on the Chinese Dream and China's Development Path,
https://doi.org/10.1007/978-981-13-9841-4_3

innovation should respect objective laws and make steady progress. For financial innovations with mature conditions and economic reality, we must boldly introduce and maintain the necessary international universality in business and technology innovations such as operating varieties, financial instruments, financing technologies, trading methods, and financial electronics. For financial innovations that are related to financial security, we must analyze and study from objective reality, and then bring about innovations after conditions are mature. We must not blindly copycat the innovative achievements of the developed countries.

3. The principle of government actively providing guidance. As the main entities of financial innovation, financial institutions often only see the positive effects on improving the liquidity of financial markets and the efficiency of financial resource allocation, but ignore the destructive aspects of financial innovation. As an independent regulator of the market, the government can be more rational and comprehensive in recognizing the positive and negative effects of financial innovation. Therefore, innovations actively guided by the government tend to be more robust.

4. The principle of comparative advantage. Financial innovation is a financial activity that involves a wide range o f issues. If it is pushed forward in all aspects regardless of innate conditions, the expected results cannot be achieved. Therefore, Shenzhen's financial innovation must be combined with its own advantages and characteristics.

2   Model of Shenzhen's Financial Innovation

With reference to the developmental law of international financial innovation, there are three models available for choice by Shenzhen:

1. Original innovation. This type refers to the technology innovation carried out by the innovation entity based on its independent research and development. For this kind of innovation, the financial innovation entity needs to not only invest more resources in the innovation, but also accumulate a wealth of financial theoretical knowledge, such as asset portfolio and pricing theory, binomial option pricing model and so on. Then, the new financial products can be created by virtue of certain computerized technological means. Therefore, on a global scale, the original financial innovations mostly originate from the developed countries.

2. Integrated innovation. That is to say, the innovation entity combines and optimizes various innovation elements such as technology, strategy, knowledge, organization, etc., and integrates them in the most reasonable structural form to generate innovative products with functional enhancement. It is an independent type of innovation based on the integration of systematic elements of innovation. In this kind of innovation, the innovation entity can take the lead in occupying the market and gain the initiative in competition if it not only gives full play to its own

technical strength and through the systematic integration of various elements and various levels of the specific goal, forms its own products in a relatively short period of time, but also fits them into its domestic brand strategy.
3. Simulating innovation. This refers to an independent type of innovation based on the introduction of technology. Its technology innovations originate from the outside rather than the inside of the system of innovation entity.

To make the choice of Shenzhen's financial innovation model, the following basic judgments need to be made. First, original innovation has the highest requirements with respect to the cost of research and the difficulty of the financial innovation entities. In the global environment of competition, Shenzhen's capabilities for independent innovation are still relatively underdeveloped. It is still difficult to gain competitive advantages through original financial innovation. Second, as compared with original innovation, integrated innovation has a lower cost, a shorter cycle and a smaller amount of risk, thus being an independent innovation with great economic value. Integrated innovation requires the comprehensive application of multiple technologies and multi-disciplines. According to its own characteristics and the experience of innovation at home and abroad, to some extent, it is feasible for Shenzhen to take the road of integrated innovation. Third, simulating innovation has the lowest requirements for the innovation entities. It is a model adopted by many late-developing countries, and also a relatively simple and rapid promotion method of financial innovation. Because the late-mover advantage of backward countries, they also have such an advantage in the financial sector. The late-developing countries learn from the developed countries, borrow various advanced financial innovation products, financial transaction rules, financial regulation systems, financial legal systems, etc., and then bring about innovations after assimilation and absorption. It is a common practice for countries and regions with relatively backward technologies in the world to achieve leap-forward development. The conclusion is that: as a test field for China's financial reform and innovation, Shenzhen should adopt the developmental model with focus on simulating innovation and supplemented by integrated innovation. The simulating kind of innovation can rapidly reduce R&D costs and increase the probability of success, and the integrated type of innovation is an effective way to gradually realize independent innovation given that original innovation is difficult.

3 Timings of Shenzhen's Financial Innovation

The timing of innovation studies what kind of financial innovation strategy can be adopted under what conditions. Financial innovation is a double-edged sword because it has both positive and negative effects. Financial entities have their trade-offs and considerations when choosing financial innovation. Some financial innovation entities perform well in fierce competition and actively innovate, but other entities may only take the follow-suit strategy because of the uncertain prospects of new products. Therefore, the initial conditions of financial innovation will have a significant influence on the effects of that innovation. According to different initial conditions, Shenzhen faces three options in advancing the process of financial innovation: First, aggressive promotion of financial innovation without initial conditions; second, advancing the financial innovation after the initial conditions are improved; and third, perfecting the initial conditions while implementing financial innovation.

In our opinion, the first option may undermine the stability of the financial system and increase social unrest. Shenzhen should not take this option. The second option, although the most secure with the least impact on the economy, is too conservative. The financial innovation begins only after the initial conditions are improved. This may miss the proper timing of financial innovation. For Shenzhen, the ideal strategy should be the third option. Shenzhen, as the most innovative special economic zone in China, has the advantage of the first pilot and first trial policy, so it can speed up the pace of financial innovation. At the same time, the test results of Shenzhen's financial innovation will not have a devastating impact on the steady operation of the country's entire financial system.

4 Ideas of Shenzhen's Financial Innovation

In accordance with the current conditions, the ideas of Shenzhen's financial innovation should be carried out by centering on the following five aspects:

1. Important tasks of the national financial reform. There are two urgent issues in China's future financial reforms: The first is the internationalization of the RMB; and the second is the marketization of interest rates. The former is to allow the Chinese economy to be integrated into the existing world financial trading system as soon as possible, while the latter is to allow the rigid financial market to adapt to the changing needs of the real economy as quickly as possible. As a pioneer in China's economic and financial system reform, Shenzhen must be at the forefront of the country. On the one hand, it explores the convertibility of RMB capital accounts on the platform of Qianhai and finds a path for the RMB to become an international means of payment and storage; on the other hand, it builds a flexible financial market to strengthen the risk tolerance of financial institutions, while offering enterprises with more convenient and low-cost financing instruments.

2. Distinctive advantages of Shenzhen. Now the distinctive advantages of Shenzhen's financial innovation can be summarized as three points: First, a multi-layered capital market unique in China; second, the international financial center of Hong Kong; and third, highly developed high-tech industries. If Shenzhen's financial innovation can firmly grasp these three threads, it can take the lead in this round of domestic financial innovation.

3. Satisfying the market needs. The financial sector of Shenzhen must conscientiously do well in the survey and analysis of the market and customer needs in the special economic zone. On the one hand, it is necessary to create new

financial institutions based on the objective needs of the real economy. On the other hand, new financial products must be designed according to the actual conditions of enterprises, such as production and operation characteristics, project cash flow cycle, and the borrowers' application of funds. On this basis, a highly efficient financial market is formed to ensure that the funds can be allocated to the industries and enterprises that are most in need.

4. Increase in added value. Shenzhen's financial innovation should not just focus on the growth of scale and size of the society and its own, but also pursue the value increase and new value creation. To this end, the results of financial innovation, on the one hand, should be conducive to increasing revenue and efficiency for customers; on the other hand, reducing operating and financial costs for innovation entities and enhancing their profitability.

5. Risk mitigation. A series of financial innovation products launched before the US subprime mortgage crisis, in the eyes of the world then, have increased the benefits of innovation entities and transferred risks. However, in fact, these products did not really resolve the risks, but only deferred and hid them. Therefore, Shenzhen's financial innovation needs to address both immediate and long-term needs. It is necessary to pursue the benefits and prevent risks throughout the entire process of financial innovation, strengthen risk management and control, and comprehensively assess the symmetry of innovation gains and costs.

5 Content of Shenzhen's Financial Innovation

According to the principles of finance, financial innovation includes at least three major structures:

1. Financial market innovation. Specific to Shenzhen, the current financial market innovation should undertake at least three primary tasks:

(1) To actively build a nationwide NEEQ (National Equities Exchange and Quotations) market. Shenzhen currently has satisfied the conditions for building a nationwide NEEQ market. First, the NEEQ market trading is currently entrusted to the Shenzhen Stock Exchange's agency share transfer system. The Shenzhen Stock Exchange assumes the function of a technology platform and has the technological advantages in opening accounts for users, daily operations of the quotation transfer system, and application for listing and delisting of companies. Second, the establishment of the SME board and second-board market volatility system in Shenzhen requires a developed national NEEQ market. Third, Shenzhen has the developed venture capitals, and the establishment of the NEEQ market can open up a new channel for the exit of venture capitals. In order to improve operational efficiency, we propose to fully introduce the market maker system in the NEEQ market. Because under the market maker system, prices quoted by the market makers are based on the comprehensive analysis of the information of all participants in the market for evaluation of their own risks

and benefits. The investors make decisions based on the quotation and then influence the quotation of market makers, so the securities prices become gradually close to their actual value. This is conducive to achieving a reasonable valuation of innovative enterprises. At the same time, market makers conduct bilateral quotations for buyers and sellers and immediately trade, thus maintaining the continuity of securities transactions and improving liquidity and market efficiency.

(2) To gradually open the international board. That is to say, an independent board is set up on the Shenzhen Stock Exchange and it opens up a special channel for overseas enterprises which wish to be listed in Shenzhen. From the perspective of mature foreign capital markets, it is a common practice to introduce high-quality overseas enterprises to be listed on the domestic exchange for making the capital market big and strong. What's more, Shenzhen already meets the conditions for opening the international board, such as technology, laws, policies and market capacity. In particular, under the *Guangdong-Hong Kong Cooperation Framework Agreement*, qualified enterprises should be encouraged to be listed cross-border on the second-board markets of Shenzhen and Hong Kong. This provides a policy basis for the Shenzhen Stock Exchange to open an international board. It should be pointed out that in order to avoid homogenous competition with the Shanghai Stock Exchange, the international board of the Shenzhen Stock Exchange should pay more attention to international high-quality SMEs with good prospects when selecting listed companies.

(3) To establish an offshore financial center in due course. Objectively speaking, Shenzhen cannot fully satisfy some rigid conditions for setting up an offshore financial center, such as foreign exchange marketization, capital account convertibility and effective regulation systems. However, Shenzhen is currently the most promising region in China that can have a first try as an offshore financial center for the following reasons. First, Shenzhen is the first pilot city in China to launch the offshore asset business with relevant experience and talents for developing offshore business. Second, Shenzhen is adjacent to the Hong Kong International Finance Centre and can easily absorb the success of Hong Kong's financial sector in developing offshore financial services. Third, the RMB business is developing rapidly in Hong Kong. If an offshore financial center is established in the process of constructing an RMB reflow mechanism, it will make sure that the offshore financial market quickly takes shape. Of course, to become successful on the first try of the construction of an offshore financial center, Shenzhen still needs hard work. First, we must actively seek the support of the central government, so that Shenzhen can relax foreign exchange controls and implement flexible financial policies and special tax policies. Second, it is necessary to build an internal and external separation type offshore center. During the initial stage, the domestic financial market and the offshore central market should be strictly separated, that is, the onshore and offshore business accounts should be managed separately to reduce the impact of overseas financial fluctuations on the domestic market. Third, the early offshore financial business pilot should be confined to the traditional bank deposit and loan

business and traditional stock, futures, bonds and other businesses, and should not include businesses of financial derivatives. Fourth, to strengthen the regulation of offshore financial services, and combat money laundering, tax evasion and cross-border economic crimes. The competent authorities should cooperate with international anti-financial criminal organizations and take necessary monitoring measures. The background survey is essential upon registration of companies; if a company account is suspected of money laundering or other illegal financial activities, the offshore company information must be compulsorily disclosed; if there is any evidence that a company is committing illegal activities, the company will be deregistered and the illegal funds will be recovered. The loose offshore environment should not become a "hotbed" of money laundering, fraud, and financial risks.

2. Financial product innovation. Shenzhen's financial product innovation can have good prospects in at least the following three aspects:

(1) To actively set up a venture capital guiding fund. The venture capital guiding fund is a policy fund contributed by the government to guide private funds in establishing various commercial venture capital funds. It can provide startup funds, credit guarantees, risk subsidies and relevant preferential policies for venture capital institutions and start-ups, thus effectively overcoming the market failure problem of simply arranging venture capital through the market. In order to make sure that this product can grow strong in Shenzhen, first, it is necessary to establish an effective internal management mechanism, clarify the responsibilities of all parties involved in the specific operations of the venture capital guiding fund, guide the fund not to interfere with the investment decisions and specific operations of the participating venture capital enterprises, and avoid overstepping power and evolving into a profitable organization. Second, to broaden the source of funds for venture capital guiding funds. The source of funds can be either the government's science and technology funds, state-owned capital or private capital. Third, in the use of funds, mainly to support private capitals to establish new commercial venture capital enterprises by means of shareholding. Venture capital enterprises of good credit standing can be provided with financing guarantees to support their capability of enhancing investment through debt financing. Fourth, in management, to establish an effective income incentive mechanism and risk-constraining mechanism, and meanwhile reduce the risk of guiding funds. The guiding fund participates in the stockholding as the stockholder of preferred stocks. The applicable dividend rate can refer to the interest rate of the treasury bonds in the same period. Fifth, in terms of investment scope, to encourage priority investment in local high-tech enterprises. At the same time, high-quality enterprises that are not located in Shenzhen can also be invested in by venture capitals, so as to increase the scope of investment in excellent enterprises and improve the profitability of the fund.

(2) To launch real estate investment trust funds in due course. Real Estate Investment Trusts (REITs) refer to the trust investment method of funds by the trust company through formulating the trust plan, signing investment plans with trustees, issuing trust beneficiary certificates or stocks, making investment in real estate

or real estate mortgage loans, and entrusting and hiring a professional management team for specific business operations and management. REITs originated in the United States of America. Due to their strong liquidity, high rate of return, and tax preferences, after decades of development, REITs have become a very mature and reliable investment tool around the world. More than 20 countries and regions have launched REITs. From our point of view, the conditions are mature to launch real estate investment trusts in Shenzhen for the following reasons. First, there are supporting state policies. In 2008, the General Office of the State Council issued the *Several Opinions on Promoting the Healthy Development of the Real Estate Market* and clearly stated that "the pilot of real estate investment trusts" was launched to provide funding sources for security housing and low-rent housing. Because of the huge investments in social security housing and the long payback period, many real estate enterprises or private capital are reluctant to get involved in this field, and REITs can provide them with stable and long-term funding sources. Second, there are private guarantees. At present, the channels for Shenzhen residents to invest in are as narrow as those of the whole country, but the accumulation of private wealth is more than that of other regions. Moreover, because the real estate trust funds have professional investment management teams, they can absorb scattered residents' funds and change the speculative atmosphere of real estate speculators. This is conducive to the change in the residents' investment model. Therefore, Shenzhen should actively facilitate the development of real estate investment trusts. In order to ensure the orderly advancement of this innovation, on the one hand, we must speed up the construction of relevant laws and regulations. For example, regarding tax incentives, foreign countries allocate the high proportion of REITs' dividends to investors. There is no corporate income tax. Only investors are taxed and the tax rate is low, and this is good for investors to increase their income. On the other hand, it is necessary to strengthen the construction of the regulation system, which includes strict oversight of the establishment, structure, investment assets, income distribution and exit mechanism of REITs. Especially on the subjects of investment, foreign REITs mainly invest in commercial real estate (office buildings, shopping centers, etc.) with a long payback period and a stable income. On this basis, Shenzhen can attempt to increase its investment in government affordable housing projects and strictly restrict the investment in the commodity housing market to avoid speculation.

(3) To issue treasury bonds and foreign exchange futures options. From the macro environment and sequential experience of financial product innovation in the Western developed countries, the earliest innovation began with agricultural futures. With the marketized development of the interest rate and the exchange rate, it gradually developed towards financial futures options. China's financial derivatives have relatively few varieties, and there are currently stock index futures, treasury bond forwards, and foreign exchange forwards. The timing of launching interest-related derivatives (treasury bond futures options) and foreign exchange-related derivatives (foreign exchange futures options) is not mature, which is closely related to the two important factors that China is lacking in

interest rate liberalization and foreign exchange marketization. However, with the marketization of interest rates and the acceleration of the internationalization of the RMB, Shenzhen should be prepared for the launch of interest rate derivatives and foreign exchange derivatives.

3. Innovation of financial institutions. Shenzhen can explore financial institution innovation in the following two aspects:

(1) To actively establish securities finance companies, which, known as securities financing companies, refer to legal persons established in accordance with the law and specialized in securities financing business on the securities market, and whose main functions are absorbing deposits from commercial banks, securities companies, stock exchanges or other institutions, and lending out the funds and securities needed for credit exchanges to securities institutions. From the perspective of global experience, the development of securities finance companies has two models. First, the Japanese model. In Japan, three specialized securities finance companies act as intermediaries. Securities companies, separate from banks in securities mortgage financing, strictly control the multiplication effect of funds and securities through credit transactions, and occupy a monopolistic position. In other words, securities companies provide the credit for margin trading and securities lending to customers. When their own funds or borrowing sources are insufficient, customers will turn to securities finance companies; if securities finance companies have insufficient funds or securities, they borrow from the commercial banks, lending market, and open market operations to obtain capital inflows and outflows that regulate the securities market. Second, the Taiwan model. In Taiwan, securities finance companies implement a "dual track system" for simultaneous financing and securities lending to securities companies and general investors. Any securities company that obtains a margin trading and securities lending license can provide customers with margin trading and securities lending services, and then lend from a securities finance company. Those without such a license can only accept the customers' entrustment and apply for financing from securities finance companies on behalf o f their customers. In this way, securities finance companies actually handle the transfer of securities for some securities companies, and also directly provide margin trading and securities lending services for general investors.

In comparison, an important starting point of the Japanese model is that credit transactions can be controlled by the government as much as possible, which is conducive to controlling credit trading volume and macro-control. The Taiwan model, on the one hand, inherits the Japanese model of specialized finance companies, which takes the form of specialized centralized credit, and on the other hand, breaks through the closed mode of "institution-to-institution" in Japan, and extends the scope of margin trading and securities lending from specialized finance companies to all investors, thus realizing the direct provision of margin trading and securities lending business to both securities companies and the general investors, in an effort to fully demonstrate the characteristics of market competition in all aspects.

Given that the development of Shenzhen's capital market is still in its infancy, the market operation mechanism and laws and regulations are still not perfect. It is recommended that the Japanese model should be adopted in the near future. The establishment of securities finance companies can not only solve the problem of financing difficulties of securities companies, but also enable the competent authorities to understand the margin trading and securities lending situation of the entire market and complete the margin trading and securities lending business of securities companies under the supervision of regulatory authorities, so as to facilitate oversight and reduce risks. However, in the long run, it is necessary to transition to the Taiwan model. Because only by breaking the closed mechanism of "institution-to-institution" can the margin trading and securities lending business really grow big. Nowadays, in order to make up for the shortage of the closed mechanism of "institution-to-institution", we should vigorously expand the channels for raising funds of securities finance companies. In addition to attracting commercial banks, stock exchanges, insurance companies, investment companies, trust companies, securities companies and other financial institutions, we should also attract industrial and private capitals to participate by shareholding.

(2) To establish a bank of technology in due course. Shenzhen, an important city for China's high-tech development, has already laid a foundation for the development of a bank of technology. By the end of 2011, Shenzhen had cumulatively granted a total of 178,426 patents and 40,495 domestic effective invention patents, ranking second among large and medium-sized cities in China; the average number of invention patents per 10,000 people is 39 pieces, and the patent density ranks top. In 2011, Shenzhen's PCT international patent applications were 7933 pieces, ranking first in the country for eight consecutive years. With the continuous industrial upgrading, high-tech enterprises in Shenzhen will become more and more numerous, but these enterprises, especially small and medium-sized ones, are mostly innovative enterprises at high risks. It is difficult for them to obtain the support of commercial bank loans, which are granted solely for the purposes of avoiding risks and making profits. Therefore, Shenzhen should learn from the experience of the US Silicon Valley Bank and set up a bank of technology serving high-tech enterprises and broadening their financing channels.

Guo Maojia male, born in Wuxue, Hubei Province, Professor of China Center for Special Economic Zone Research, Shenzhen University, Ph.D., with research interests in financial theories and capital market research.

Chapter 4
On the Exploration and Practice of Social Construction in Shenzhen in the Last 30 Years

Yang Lixun

Abstract This paper systematically sorts out and summarizes the performance and experience of social construction work in the 30 years since the founding of the Shenzhen Special Economic Zone, with a focus on the improvement of people's livelihood, continuous advancement of the reform of the social system and social management innovation, achievement of a good social environment and initial construction of a new model in conformity with Shenzhen's reality. Finally, the policy suggestions are given in terms of tracking potential risk points and perfecting long-term mechanisms.

Keywords Shenzhen special economic zone · Social construction · Social management

Economic construction should "bake a bigger cake", but social construction should "divide the cake more fairly". Economic construction creates GDP, and social construction transforms GDP into GNH (Gross National Happiness) and provides a good social environment for economic development. In the past 30 years since the establishment of the Shenzhen Special Economic Zone, its social construction has made considerable progress, and initially explores a new model with Chinese characteristics and in conformity with Shenzhen's reality.

Y. Lixun (✉)
Institute of Social Development, The Shenzhen Academy
of Social Sciences, Shenzhen 518060, Guangdong, China
e-mail: szyanglixun@163.com

© Social Sciences Academic Press 2020
Y. Yuan (ed.), *Studies on China's Special Economic Zones 3*,
Research Series on the Chinese Dream and China's Development Path,
https://doi.org/10.1007/978-981-13-9841-4_4

1   In the Past 30 Years, Shenzhen Has Continuously Accelerated Its Social Construction with Focus on the Improvement of People's Livelihood, so that the Border Town Which Was Poor and Backward in the Past Has Developed into a City of Civilization, Happiness and Harmony with a Population of over 10 Million and Has Created a Good Social Environment for Advancing Scientific Development

1. **Adhering to the people-oriented philosophy, the city guarantees and improves the people's livelihood and makes great progress in the construction of a happy and livable city.** In the 30 years since the establishment of the Shenzhen Special Economic Zone, it has been continuously innovating the supply mode of public services, improving the public service system, implementing the white paper system of public services, introducing the evaluation system of the net welfare of people's livelihood, and thus ensuring institutionalization, refinement and long-term development of the people's work for their livelihood. For 10 consecutive years, the author has tracked 11 indicators, including "per capita disposable income of residents", "Engel's coefficient", "per capita housing area", "per capita road area", "the number of public transportation vehicles per 10,000 people", "the number of emergency vehicles per 50,000 people", "the number of community health service centers", "the number of doctors per 10,000 people" and "the number of hospital beds per 10,000 people". The results of the evaluation show that the average happiness index of Shenzhen citizens increased by 3.05% from 2001 to 2010.[1] The positive increase of 11 indicators for 10 consecutive years indicates that the people-oriented governance philosophy has been transformed into people's livelihood and welfare, and the GDP has been sublimated into GNH (Gross National Happiness).

2. **Shenzhen explores social legislation and regulates social behaviors, and hence the civilized city construction has achieved remarkable results.** Shenzhen fully utilizes the legislative power and takes the lead in carrying out experimentation of social legislation. It successively formulates the *Regulations on Blood Donation of Citizens and Blood Management of the Shenzhen Special Economic Zone*, the *Regulations on Human Organ Donation and Transplantation in the Shenzhen Special Economic Zone*, the *Regulations of Shenzhen Municipality on Volunteer Service*, the *Regulations of the Shenzhen Special Economic Zone on the Security of Wages Owed by Enterprises* and other laws and regulations. Shenzhen has established legal guarantee mechanisms such as voluntary blood donation, organ donation and volunteer services. There emerges a large series of models of morality, such as warm-hearted citizen Cong Fei, good doctor Guo Chunyuan wholeheartedly serving the people, Chen Guanyu, the Living

---

[1]Data source: Annual Evaluation and Analysis of the Shenzhen Civilization Index, project funded by Shenzhen Publicity and Culture Development Special Fund in 2011 (No. ND-2011-00353).

Lei Feng in Zhongying Street, and "Warm Love" Zeng Liuying. The whole city
has over 200 charitable organizations, and more than 200,000 registered volunteers. In 2005 and 2009, Shenzhen won the honor of national civilization city
twice. In 10 consecutive years, the author has tracked 14 indicators, including
"sales revenue of welfare lottery", "the number of people receiving legal aid",
"the number of registered volunteers", "the number of employed disabled people", "accessibility rate of barrier-free facilities in public places", "the number
of times of social assistance", "the number of welfare beds for a hundred elderly
people", "the resettlement rate of released criminals", "the rate of collection of
social insurance funds", "the payment of salaries of unpaid employees", "the
number of registrations for adoption", "the number of blood donors", "the number of cornea donors" and "the number of voluntary body donors". The results
of the evaluation show that: the love index of Shenzhen increased by 4.95%
annually from 2001 to 2010.[2] Shenzhen has become a veritable city of love and
civilization.

3. **The city carries out the peace building activity, heightens the sense of security of the people, and makes new progress in the construction of a safe city**.
   In the past 30 years, Shenzhen has continuously improved its social security network and has built a "big security" work pattern. Regarding social security, it has
   implemented the comprehensive management responsibility check system and
   grid police, promoted the "courtyard style", "property style" and "travel style"
   management mode in urban villages and "manages people by house"; for letters
   and visits and stability maintenance, the letters and visits halls are arranged at
   the city and district level, the comprehensive stability maintenance centers have
   been established at the sub-district level, and the party representative, deputy to
   the people's congress and CPPCC member work offices have been set up at the
   community level for smoothing out the public opinion expression mechanism;
   with respect to the safety of production, it has adopted a system of responsibility
   for strict production safety, it has strengthened traffic, fire prevention, explosion-
   proof safety monitoring, and is focusing on the safety management in high-risk
   areas such as urban villages; regarding food and drug safety, it has explored the
   "big oversight" pattern, set up the market supervision bureau, started the five
   projects, including soybean processing and production bases, the reform of the
   system of fixed-point slaughtering of hogs and meat circulation, canteen rectifi-
   cation and construction in industrial areas, food circulation modernization and
   agricultural product base construction, and it has regulated the advertisements of
   clinics, medical devices and drugs. In 10 consecutive years, the author has tracked
   11 indicators, including "the number of public security cases", "the number of
   criminal cases", "the number of traffic accidents", "the number of fire accidents",
   "the incidence rate of infectious diseases", "the food and drug safety accident
   rate" and so on. The results of the evaluation show that: the security index of
   Shenzhen increased by 2.89% annually from 2001 to 2010[3] and has kept a good

---

[2] See Footnote 1.
[3] See Footnote 1.

trend of "small steps but fast running" for 10 years. The construction of a peaceful city has achieved good results.

4. **Shenzhen implements the strategy of the culture-based city, protects citizens' cultural rights and interests and constantly enhances its soft power**. The successive municipal party committees and city governments give great importance to the construction of cultural soft power and a smart city, continuously intensify the reform of the cultural management system, vigorously support the creation of excellent cultural products, introduce and cultivate cultural talents, establish and perfect the public cultural service system, and continually satisfy the basic cultural needs of the citizens. The cultural products are resounding all over the country, such as the "Story of Spring", "Enter the New Era" and "Road to Rejuvenation". The "Citizen Culture Lecture Hall" and "24-hour Self-service Library" have won the National Cultural Innovation Award. The "Reading Month" improves the reading habits of this city. Shenzhen has won the honors of "Leading Region of Cultural System Reform of China" and "Leading City of Ideological and Moral Construction of Underage People". The cultural industry is also undergoing great development. "Culture + Capital" and "Culture + Technology" make the cultural industry even more powerful. The amount of transactions of the "Cultural Industry Fair" continuously updates its historical record, and the proportion of the output value of the cultural industry to the GDP is continuously increasing. In 10 consecutive years, the author has tracked 12 indicators, including "total science, education, culture and health expenses expressed as a percentage of financial expenditures", "total public expenditure on education expressed as a percentage of GDP", "per capita expenditures for science popularization activities", "proportion of output value of cultural industry to GDP", "per capita education, culture and entertainment consumption expenditures", "promotion rate of senior secondary school graduates", "the number of books in public libraries per capita", "the number of Internet users per 100 people", "the area of per capita public sports facilities", "the number of scientific and technological research results", "the number of patent applications per 10,000 people" and "the number of people with a college education or above per 10,000 people". The results of the evaluation show that the average cultural index of Shenzhen increased by 16.17% annually from 2001 to 2010.[4] This indicates that the momentum of development of Shenzhen transitions from reliance on hard power to soft power. The transformation of the developmental model has made remarkable achievements.

5. **The city builds a credit evaluation management system, cultivates a contract-honoring culture, and takes new steps in constructing a creditworthy city**. Shenzhen takes the lead in exploring corporate credit and personal credit evaluation management methods, establishing the government public credit service platform, and opening the corporate credit information service network integrating more than 30 government departments and covering more than 700,000 market entities. The personal credit information system is networked with the

---

[4]See Footnote 1.

National Citizen Identity Information Center, government departments, commercial banks, and national credit card center. The city has issued the *Implementation Opinions of Shenzhen on the Sunshine Project*, it is promoting the "seven disclosures" of party, government, legal, school, medical, residence and enterprise affairs, and is trying to build a creditworthy party organization, government, court, school and enterprises. In 10 consecutive years, the author has tracked 11 indicators, including "the number of unfair competition cases per 10,000 people", "the number of cases of production and sale of counterfeit and shoddy commodities per 10,000 people", "the number of smuggling cases per 10,000 people", "the number of trademark infringement cases per 10,000 people", "the number of unlicensed clinics per 10,000 people", "the conformity rate of food hygiene", "the number of arbitration cases for labor disputes per 10,000 people", "the number of investigated cases of wages in arrears", "the number of cases of recovering wages in arrears", "the number of traffic violations per 10,000 people" and "the clearance of unpaid taxes by local and state taxations". The results of the evaluation show that the credibility index of Shenzhen increased by 5.46% annually from 2001 to 2010, and so maintained a positive growth for 10 consecutive years. The creditworthy city construction has found a new path.

6. **The city establishes the anti-corruption and incorruptible system, ensures that public power is exercised transparently, and makes initial achievements in the construction of a clean city**. The Municipal Party Committee and the Municipal Government implement the "Responsibility Storm" and "Mediocre Treatment Plan", issue the "1+6" document to strengthen the building of the ability to govern, and formulate the *Implementation Opinions on Establishing and Perfecting the System of Punishing and Preventing Corruption with Equal Stress on Education, System and Oversight*, the *Opinions on Further Strengthening the Construction of a Clean and Honest Culture*, and the *Decision on Building a Clean City*. The administrative service hall has been established for "one window to the outside", "one-stop office" and "one-stop service". It simplifies administrative reviews and approvals, develops an electronic system for administrative approvals, monitors the entire process of administrative approvals, and ensures where the public authority runs, where there is monitoring, where the financial funds are used, where there is audit and where the public service is provided, where there is performance evaluation. In 10 consecutive years, the author has tracked 6 indicators, including "the number of corruption and bribery cases filed by the public procuratorate against civil servants", "the number of cases of prosecution against civil servants for dereliction of duty", "the number of cases of administrative disputes accepted by courts against civil servants", "the number of disciplinary actions by discipline inspection and supervisory organs against civil servants", and "the number of administrative errors and administrative effectiveness of civil servants". The results of the evaluation show that the incorruptibility index of Shenzhen increased annually by 4.35% from 2001 to 2010,[5] and the construction of a clean city has begun to bear fruits.

---

[5] See Footnote 1.

7. **The city places the construction of a resource-saving and environment-friendly society in a prominent position within the strategy of industrialization and urbanization, and reaches a new stage in the construction of an ecological city**. It has issued a series of local laws and regulations on environmental protection, formulated basic regulations for the management of the ecological control line, prepared the plans for the building of an ecological demonstration city and included nearly half of the city's land in the ecological control line for strict protection. The city has taken the environment improvement action plan and issued the *Decision on Improving the Quality of Urban Development*, is severely curbing the destruction of forests for planting fruit trees, illegal quarrying and development, over-exploitation and illegal construction, it is treating pollution with an iron hand, repels pollution with an iron law and protects the environment with an iron line. It has won the titles of "National Health City", "National Garden City", "National Green Model City", "National Environmental Protection Model City", "International Garden City" and has been included in the "Global Environment Top 500". In 10 consecutive years, the author has tracked 10 indicators, including "proportion of green space in built-up district", "per capita public green space area", "environmental protection investment index", "the rate of treatment of harmless waste", "the rate of centralized treatment of domestic sewage", "the rate of compliance to industrial wastewater discharge norms", "days of air quality reaching national first and second-class standards during the whole year", "the rate of compliance with industrial soot emission norms", "rate of compliance with noise level standards" and "the rate of compliance with the standards of water quality of the reservoirs of the source of drinking water". The results of the evaluation show that the ecological index of Shenzhen increased annually by 3.96% from 2001 to 2010.[6] The construction of an ecological environment is improving year by year.

---

[6]Data source: Annual Evaluation and Analysis of the Shenzhen Civilization Index, project funded by Shenzhen Publicity and Culture Development Special Fund in 2011.

2   In the Past 30 Years, Shenzhen Continuously Carried Out the Reform of the Social System and Social Management Innovation, It Explored the Long-Term Mechanism of the Work on Social Construction, and Initially Formed the New Social Construction Model that Reflects the Laws of Social Development, Has Chinese Characteristics, and Coincides with the Reality of Shenzhen

1. **The city has perfected the system of organization and leadership and promoted the long-term work on social construction.** The Municipal Party Committee and the Municipal Government treat social construction in an equally important way as economic construction, they hold the conference on the work on social construction, they have established the leading group of work on Shenzhen social construction, and formulated the *Decisions of the Shenzhen Municipal Party Committee and the People's Government of Shenzhen on Strengthening Social Construction*, the *Social Construction Evaluation Index System of Shenzhen*, and the *Five-Year Action Plan for the Social Construction of Shenzhen*. They clearly propose to improve people's livelihood, bring about innovations to social management, strengthen community services, foster social organizations, perfect the quality of their citizens, intensify the reform, enhance organizational leadership and reinforce studies on social construction, thus forming synergy and an atmosphere of social construction, and comprehensively and systematically advancing the work on social construction of the city.

2. **It explores the index monitoring mechanism and facilitates scientific work on social construction.** The city issues the citizen net welfare index system and releases the Shenzhen Civilization Index consisting of seven primary indexes of a love index, a credibility index, a cultural index, a happiness index, a security index, an incorruptibility index and an ecological index as well as 75 secondary indexes. It formulates the government performance evaluation system so that the government can be evaluated and the officials can be examined. The city studies and devises the harmonious Shenzhen evaluation system, regularly conducts the citizen happiness and social opinion surveys, promptly understands the situation of social development and the needs of citizens, provides scientific reference for the formulation of social policies, and advances the scientific and refined work on social construction.

3. **The city actively explores the legislative guarantee mechanism and facilitates the standardization of the work on social construction.** Since being granted legislative power in 1992, Shenzhen continuously fixes the innovation results and experience of social construction in legal forms, and promotes its sustainable and healthy development. For example, the legislation practices on social security, labor and employment, talents and personnel, education and training, voluntary blood donation, organ donation, volunteer services, guarantee for wage arrears,

labor relations, smoking control, medical assistance and population management, plays the roles of radiation, demonstration and driving for the legislation in the social fields across the country.

4. **It innovates the grassroots management methods and boosts the networking of the work on social construction**. In the past 30 years, Shenzhen has continuously brought about innovations to the administrative management system and social management methods at the grassroots level. In order to divest the administrative functions of the neighborhood committees and enhance the grassroots social management and public service platform, the community workstations are set up to specifically undertake the administrative services of public security, sanitation, population, family planning, culture, law, environment, science and education, civil affairs, employment, stability maintenance and management of retirees from government departments. The city vigorously advances the "weaving network project", accelerates the construction of comprehensive community service centers, comprehensively integrates the community work network, management network, service network and mediation network, forms the administrative service system led by community party organizations on the community workstations and the grassroots self-governance system of community-based neighborhood committees, and promotes the networking of social construction.

5. **The city brings about innovations to the supervision of social organizations and diversifies the entities for social construction**. Social organizations are essential for building a harmonious society, expanding the participation of the masses, reflecting the demands of the masses, enhancing the functions of social autonomy, and resolving conflicts and disputes. In the past 30 years, Shenzhen has constantly reformed the social organization registration management system through successively exploring the methods of direct registration of industry associations, of no competent authorities of industry associations and non-governmentalization of industry associations. It has adopted the direct registration system for social welfare and charitable social organizations, and introduced the interim measures for the registration of chambers of commerce in other regions. The city has broadened the communication platform between the government and social organizations, organized the social organizations to participate in various hearings and demonstrations, established social organization incubation platforms and incubation experiment bases, and has promoted the transfer of government functions to social organizations. The government purchases services from social organizations and expands the room for their development. By the end of 2010, there were more than 4100 social organizations in the city, with an average annual growth rate of 15%. In 2009, the reform of the management of social organization registration of Shenzhen won the "China's Local Government Innovation Award".

6. **It improves the mechanism for safeguarding rights and interests and promotes the popularization of basic public services**. In the past 30 years, Shenzhen has built multi-level social safety networks, improved the systems of pensions, medical care, unemployment, work-related injury and maternity medical insurance and has made the people safe; moreover, it has strengthened food and

drug safety supervision and has reassured the people, it has improved public health and the system of epidemic prevention and made the people healthy; in addition, it has enhanced the comprehensive management of public security, made the people peaceful, reinforced the supervision of production safety and made the city safe; Shenzhen has also established an emergency response system and made the society stable, built a multi-channel social consultation network, improved the big mediation mechanism, the tripartite consultation mechanism of labor relations, the community consultation mechanism, the public decision consultation mechanism, the hearing mechanism of important livelihood projects, and the risk assessment mechanism of reform and legislation, and it has resolved social contradictions and disputes at the source, built a comprehensive social assistance network, and constantly brought about improvements to the minimum living security, medical assistance, education assistance, homeless assistance, legal aid and other mechanisms to achieve multi-level cross-sectoral joint assistance.

7. **The city has established a linking mechanism of "social workers" and "volunteers" to enable the seamless connection of social work**. It has promulgated the *Opinions of the Shenzhen Municipal Party Committee and People's Government on Strengthening the Building up of a Social Work Talent Team and Advancing the Development of Social Work* (referred to as the "1+7" document) and constructed a modern social work system characterized by government encouragement and private operations. There are more than 1000 full-time social workers and over 40 professional social work institutions in the city offering services for the young and the old, women and children, rehabilitation, social assistance, labor employment, drug rehabilitation, community correction and other groups. It has formulated the *Implementation Plan for Linking Social Workers and Volunteers in their Work*, it has built a four-level volunteer service network from city, districts, sub-districts to communities, established the mechanism for linking up social workers and volunteers, constructed a linkage platform, formed the social work network by social workers leading volunteers and volunteers guiding other parties, and it has allowed for the seamless connection of the professionalization and socialization of social work. Shenzhen has thus won the honor of becoming a "National Social Work Pilot Demonstration City".

8. **It brings about innovations to the grassroots governance model and facilitates continuous optimization of the community governance structure**. In order to adapt to the situation of increasing the migrant population, Shenzhen takes the lead in renaming the residents' committee to be the community residents' committee and includes the migrant population in the scope of community management services. To heighten their sense of belonging, all the members of the community residents' committee are directly elected and the non-resident population has been granted the right to elect and be elected. For the separation of enterprises and society, the community collective stock companies are delinked from the community residents' committee, so that the companies can concentrate on economic work and the committee may focus on residents' autonomy and community services. In order to explore the separation of community

administrative power and autonomy, the community workstations are set up to take over the administrative power, and the community residents' committees retain their autonomous power. Finally, it has shaped a governance model of joint consultation and construction and sharing the community among community workstations, community residents' committees, owners' committees, property management companies, enterprises and social organizations in the area.

3   The Next 30 Years Are an Important Strategic Period for Shenzhen to Achieve Scientific Development, and also a Period Full of Social Contradictions and Problems. The Key Points of the Work on Social Construction Are a Timely Check of Social Risk Points and Improvement of the Mechanisms of Mass Expression, Interest Coordination, Contradiction Settlement and the Protection of Rights, to Resolve Social Contradictions and Problems at the Source

1. **The potential risk points that affect social harmony and stability must be discovered promptly and studied in advance**. In particular, we must pay special attention to and follow up the following six potential risk points. **First**, the political risk point, which is mainly caused by the corruption and the consequences of which are the damage to the relationship between the party and the masses, the cadres and the masses, and finally the death of core values and beliefs; **second**, the economic risk point, which mainly comes from a high unemployment rate and high inflation rate and the consequences of which are the increase in the misery index of social members and social turmoil; **third**, the social risk point, which is mainly due to the continuous expansion of the Gini coefficient and advancing beyond the point of social tolerance, the consequences of which are the relative sense of deprivation and the resulting psychological tension and imbalance of the majority of the members of society; **fourth**, the regional risk point, which mainly derives from the widening development gap within and outside the special economic zone, the consequence of which is the conflict between the polarized areas; **fifth**, the population structure risk point, which is mainly due to the long-term inversion of household registered population and non-registered population, the consequence of which is the conflict between the household registered group and the non-household registered group; **sixth**, the labor relationship risk point, which is mainly caused by mass incidents as a result of there not being equal pay for equal work, or same hours for same work and nor same rights for same work of migrant workers. Any of the above six risk points can directly affect the harmony and stability of Shenzhen. What is even more terrifying is the multiplier effect released by the superposition of the six risk points, which will lead

to serious social conflicts. Therefore, the focus of Shenzhen's work on social construction in the future is to promptly discover and resolve the points of social risk.

2. **Shenzhen must establish and improve the long-term mechanism to enable social harmony and stability**. **First**, to establish and improve the regional coordinated development mechanism, speed up the process of integration of the special economic zone, and boost the balanced and coordinated development of all areas of the city. **Second**, to establish and improve the basic public service system, solve the dual employment system, dual education system and dual welfare system with household registration as the core, weave a social security network for disadvantaged groups through public power, public resources and a social security system, and advocate social fairness and justice. **Third**, to establish and improve the open social mobility mechanism, provide the people with opportunities for promotion through smooth vertical mobility, widen the room for their development through smooth horizontal mobility, and eliminate the barriers, frictions and conflicts among social members. **Fourth**, to optimize and perfect the social structure, increase the proportion of middle-income groups, and transform the "dumbbell-shaped" social structure into an "olive-shaped" social structure. **Fifth**, to accelerate the development of social organizations, make full use of their functions of services, coordination, ties, supervision, stability, etc., and resolve social conflicts and disputes. **Sixth**, to improve the structure of income distribution and the mechanism of interest coordination. The primary distribution dominated by the market should highlight efficiency, the secondary distribution dominated by the government should lay stress on fairness, and the tertiary distribution dominated by charitable organizations should pay attention to humanity. They constitute a structure of uniform social distribution of efficiency, fairness and humanity so that all of the people can share the results of development. **Seventh**, to establish and improve the mechanisms of the expression of appeal and of contradiction coordination, perfect the social governance structure, comprehensively use self-discipline and discipline by others, social management and administrative management, cohesiveness of core values and tolerance of multiculturalism, and effectively guide and reduce social contradictions and disputes. **Eighth**, to establish and improve the social early warning mechanism, the mechanism for public opinion collection and analysis and social emergency response mechanism, regularly evaluate the social harmony index and use it as an important basis for observing the "barometer" of the society and formulating social policies, thus promoting the work on scientific social construction.

Yang Lixun Deputy Director of the Shenzhen Reform Office, researcher, with research interests in urban development, social construction and social management issues.

Chapter 5
Research on the Response Mechanism of Legislation Evaluation of China's Special Economic Zone

Song Ming and Chen Jialin

Abstract The purpose of the evaluation of the legislation of the Shenzhen Special Economic Zone is to achieve the "assurance of legislative quality" and guide the "enaction, amendment and abolition" of regulations. However, in the practice of the evaluation of legislation, there is a clear disconnection between the evaluation work and the evaluation response. It is entirely up to the subjective attitude of the evaluated subjects on whether to respond to the problems identified in the evaluation, hence the evaluation of the legislation becomes formalistic. In order to guarantee the realization of the purpose of the system of evaluation of the legislation, an effective mechanism for response to the evaluation must be established to achieve the effective connection between identifying the problem and solving it.

Keywords Evaluation of SEZ legislation · Legislation quality · Evaluation response mechanism

1 Phenomena and Problems

The system of evaluation of local legislation has its origin in the Western developed countries ruled by law at the end of the 20th century. It stems from the needs of the modern society to optimize the legislative content, improve the legislative quality, and save the legislative resources. In China, since the Standing Committee of the Shandong Provincial People's Congress took the lead in delineating the "review of legislation" as the key point of work in 2000, most of the provinces and cities across the country have carried out or are conducting the post-legislation evaluation of local or government regulations. The practice of evaluating legislation in the Shenzhen Special Economic Zone (SEZ) began in 2006. In December 2006, the Standing Committee of the Shenzhen Municipal People's Congress made a law enforcement survey on the "School Safety Management Regulations of Shenzhen" by distributing questionnaires to the citizens, and this was called the "First Launch of Ex-Post

S. Ming (✉) · C. Jialin
Law School of Shenzhen University, Shenzhen 518060, China
e-mail: songmingjihai@163.com

© Social Sciences Academic Press 2020
Y. Yuan (ed.), *Studies on China's Special Economic Zones 3*,
Research Series on the Chinese Dream and China's Development Path,
https://doi.org/10.1007/978-981-13-9841-4_5

59

Legislation Evaluation in Shenzhen" by the Shenzhen Municipal People's Congress.[1] Subsequently, the Standing Committee of the Shenzhen Municipal People's Congress also evaluated the regulations such as "Regulations on the Use of Archives and Documents of the Shenzhen Special Economic Zone", Article 14 of the "Science and Technology Innovation Promotion Regulations of the Shenzhen Special Economic Zone" and "Radio Regulations (Draft) of the Shenzhen Special Economic Zone". This laid a foundation for the exploration and development of the system of evaluation of legislation in Shenzhen.

However, through investigating the work of legislation evaluation in Shenzhen, it has been found that the response mechanism of the evaluation of Shenzhen's legislation is not perfect and the response of relevant departments on the results of the evaluation of legislation depends entirely on their subjective attitudes. For example, in 2006, the Standing Committee of the Shenzhen Municipal People's Congress initiated the evaluation of the "School Safety Management Regulations of Shenzhen", and the relevant departments made a positive response to the results of the evaluation.[2] At the "Legislation Hearing of Shenzhen Municipal People's Congress on Radio Management Regulations"[3] held by the Shenzhen Municipal People's Congress in September 2008, whether the opinions and suggestions put forward at the hearing were adopted and to what extent they were adopted, the Shenzhen Municipal People's Congress made no disclosure or explanation in the follow-up work. Therefore, the evaluation of the legislation of the Shenzhen SEZ is still in the stage of preliminary exploration, especially in the setting of the mechanism of response to evaluation.

2   Significances for Perfecting the Response Mechanism of the Evaluation of the Legislation of the SEZ

The vitality of law lies in practice, and the vitality of the system of evaluation of legislation lies in the realization of "assurance of legislative quality".[4] The system of evaluation of the SEZ legislation intends to carry out the risk prediction or performance evaluation of the SEZ regulations, identify the potential risks and problems in the process of enforcement, and use the conclusions of the evaluation as the important basis for the legislative body to formulate, integrate or further amend and improve the

---

[1] See: "First Launch of Ex-Post Legislation Evaluation in Shenzhen", http://www.szlh.gov.cn.

[2] See Lin Yuanchang, "Report on the Implementation of the School Safety Management Regulations of Shenzhen", on 10th Meeting of the Standing Committee of the 4th Session of the Shenzhen Municipal People's Congress on January 18, 2007.

[3] See: "Legislation Hearing of the Shenzhen Municipal People's Congress on Radio Management Regulations", http://www.sznews.com/.

[4] See Ren Erxin, *A Study on the System of Tracking the Evaluation of Local Legislative Quality*, Peking University Press, 2010, Preface Page 1.

regulations. The mechanism of response to the evaluation, which enables the evaluation work to achieve the purpose of "assurance of legislative quality", is essential for the improvement of the SEZ regulations. "A perfect mechanism of the evaluation of legal performance should include this stage (response to the results of the evaluation of the legal performance), and it can be said that this stage is the ultimate pursuit and destination of the evaluation of legal performance."[5] It is of great significance to establish a sound mechanism of response to the evaluation of the SEZ legislation.

First, by perfecting the mechanism of response to the evaluation of legislation, the legislative quality and the legislation work of the SEZ can be improved. The laws are enacted according to the previous experience. However, due to the limited rationality of human beings and the limitations of the laws themselves, there is inevitably the possibility of legislative omissions. There is often a gap between the law's "to-be" and "ought-to-be". The same is true of the SEZ regulations. The establishment of the mechanism of response to the evaluation of the SEZ legislation can promptly control and adjust the potential legislative risks and legal regulation effects found in the evaluation, and create conditions and enrich the foundation for the formulation, continuation and improvement of the SEZ legislation. On the other hand, if we emphasize only the evaluation, but not the response to the evaluation report, then the system of evaluation of legislation will only stay at the stage of discovering the problems and cannot truly achieve its purpose and goal. This not only leads to a waste of resources, but it also cannot improve the quality of the SEZ legislation.

Second, by perfecting the mechanism of response to the evaluation of legislation, the legislation costs can be reduced and legal resources can be saved. The evaluation of the legislation includes two forms: "ex-ante evaluation" and "ex-post evaluation". "Ex-ante evaluation" refers to predicting the potential impact of legislation before the law is promulgated; "ex-post evaluation" refers to the evaluation of the regulation effects after the laws and regulations have been enforced for a period of time. The effect of regulation is evaluated. First, constructing the mechanism of response to the evaluation of the SEZ legislation and objectively analyzing and summarizing the results of the ex-ante evaluation and ex-post evaluation can reduce the cost of "trial and error" in the legislative process[6] and save legal resources. Second, the relevant state organs respond in a targeted way to the potential risks of legislation and the existing problems presented by the evaluation of legislation, which can improve the rationalization of decision-making and reduce the cost of "mandatory institutional changes".[7]

---

[5] See Wang Quansheng, *The Mechanism of Legal Performance Evaluation*, Peking University Press, 2010, pp. 13–14.

[6] See Ren Erxin, *A Study on the System of Tracking the Evaluation of Local Legislative Quality*, Peking University Press, 2010, Preface Page 2.

[7] See Zhu Suli, *Rule of Law and Its Indigenous Resources*, China University of Political Science and Law Press, 2004, pp. 3–24. According to Mr. Zhu Suli, since the late Qing Dynasty, the laws enacted in China have mostly been "designed and planned by scholars and experts who are familiar with the law theories or foreign laws" and thus are contrary to the habits of Chinese people and belonging to "mandatory institutional changes" that are not easily accepted by the people. The author believes that in such an institutional environment, in order to enforce such laws and achieve the rule of

Third, by perfecting the mechanism of response to the evaluation of legislation, the government authority can be established and a responsible government image can be built up. Although the evaluation of legislation does not necessarily have the "enaction, amendment and abolition" effects on the SEZ regulations as the objects of evaluation, the government or relevant departments can respond to the contents of the evaluation report in a timely manner, adopt the feasible suggestions in the evaluation report and take the targeted measures to control and adjust the risks and problems; and the detailed statement and explanations may be provided to those suggestions not adopted. This will not only restrict the exercise of public power, but it is also an important means to improving the efficiency and prestige of state organs.

3 Suggestions for Perfecting the Response Mechanism of the Evaluation of the Legislation of the SEZ

Completion of the evaluation report does not mean the end of the evaluation. The evaluation report only reflects the potential risks of the SEZ regulations and the problems in their enforcement, and provides a reference for the "enaction, amendment and abolition" of laws and regulations. Therefore, if the results of the evaluation are to be transformed into realistic legislative decisions, it is necessary to improve the mechanism of response of the evaluation of the SEZ's legislation.

(1) Subjects for perfecting the mechanism of response to the evaluation of the SEZ's legislation.

"The response to the results of the evaluation of legal performance actually reflects a certain legal relationship. The responding bodies are the subjects of the legal relationship of response, comprising the response subjects and the obligation subjects."[8] Furthermore, according to the evaluation time, the evaluation of the legislation can be divided into two different forms: "ex-ante evaluation" and "ex-post evaluation". The two forms are a little different in terms of the subjects of response. Accordingly, the author will make an analysis and give an explanation with the classification of the right subjects and the obligation subjects as the main clue and taking account of the specific situation of the ex-ante evaluation and the ex-post evaluation.

First, the subjects of response rights of the evaluation of SEZ legislation. Regarding the subjects of response of the system of evaluation of legislation, Mr. Wang Quansheng points out that the subjects of response rights are composed of subjects of direct rights and subjects of indirect rights. The subjects of direct rights refer to the organizations or people who directly organize, implement and participate in the

---

law, it will inevitably require more state enforcement and result in a significant increase in legal costs. On the contrary, if the mechanism of response to the evaluation of legislation is established or improved to respond to and purposefully address issues found in the evaluation of the legislation, it can narrow the gap between the enaction of laws and habits and save legal resources.

[8]See Wang Quansheng, *The Mechanism of Evaluation of Legal Performance*, Peking University Press, 2010, p. 237.

evaluation of legal performance, and the subjects of indirect rights refer to "stake-holders" that have a certain relationship with the regulations for evaluation despite no direct participation in the evaluation of legal performance.[9] The author considers that such definitions are too generalized. In fact, even the organizations or people (subjects of direct rights) who directly participate in the law and conduct the evaluation do not necessarily have the power to request the relevant authorities to respond to the evaluation. In view of China's model of evaluation of legislation dominated by the "internal evaluation" and the self-monitoring nature of the evaluation, the author defines the right subjects of the evaluation response as specific state organs which have the authority to initiate and organize the evaluations of legislation. First of all, the right subjects of the response to evaluation must be organizations that have the right to initiate and organize the evaluation of legislation, and exclude other participants such as entrusted entities,[10] invited stakeholders,[11] and so on. Second, the right subjects of the evaluation response are state organs with powers, gener-ally legislatures or their superior authorities. Since the system of the evaluation of legislation mainly conducts the forward-looking prediction or the retrospective eval-uation of the enforcement effects of the SEZ regulations to be enacted or already enacted, the initiating subjects of the system of evaluation of the SEZ legislation is generally state organs with legislative powers. To be specific, it is embodied as: the Shenzhen Municipal People's Congress and its Standing Committee have the power to conduct evaluations of the legislation of the SEZ's laws, regulations and other administrative normative documents, and they have the right to request the relevant

---

[9]See Wang Quansheng, Chen Guang, "Response Mechanism of the Results of Post-Legislation Evaluation", *Journal of Zhengzhou University (Philosophy and Social Sciences Edition)*, Jan 2011, Issue 01.

[10]For example, in the practice of evaluation of legislation of Wuhan, the Standing Committee of the Wuhan Municipal People's Congress entrusted Zhongnan University of Economics and Law on July 2, 2008 to undertake the evaluation of the existing local regulations of Wuhan, including 79 currently valid local regulations enacted by the Wuhan Municipal People's Congress and its Standing Committee from 1988 to 2008. In our opinion, although Zhongnan University of Economics and Law is the entity of participation and implementation of this evaluation, it does not have the power to require relevant authorities to respond to the conclusions of the evaluation, which always belongs to the Wuhan Municipal People's Congress and its Standing Committee.

[11]For example, the evaluation of the *Regulations of Shanghai Municipality on the Protection of the Areas with Historical Cultural Features and the Excellent Historical Buildings* was organized by the Legislative Affairs Commission of the Shanghai Municipal People's Congress and the Legal Work Sub-committee of the Standing Committee of the Shanghai Municipal People's Congress, with the participation of specialized commissions of the municipal people's congress (including legislative affairs, urban construction and environmental protection, education, science, culture and health commissions), sub-committees of the standing committee of the municipal people's congress (including legal work and personnel work committees), relevant functional departments of the municipal government (including the office of legal work, the bureau of planning, the hous-ing and land bureau, the statistics bureau and the cultural management commission), the standing committee of the district people's congress (including Huangpu District, Luwan District, Xuhui District, Changning District, Jing'an District, Hongkou District, Yangpu District and Qingpu Dis-trict) as well as invited delegates to the people's congress and experts. In this evaluation, there are many participants, but only the organizers have the power to request the evaluated agency to give a response.

authorities to respond; the Shenzhen Municipal Government has the right to evaluate the regulations and other administrative normative documents, and request the relevant authorities to respond; the city government departments, district governments and departments and the dispatching bodies have the right to conduct evaluations of the legislation on other administrative normative documents formulated by them, and request relevant bodies to respond.

Second, the subjects of response obligations of the evaluation of SEZ legislation. Regarding the obligation subjects, there are some differences between the ex-ante evaluation system and the ex-post evaluation system. The ex-ante evaluation system is mostly initiated by the legislature for the prediction of risks and improving the legislative quality. The content of the evaluation often does not involve the law enforcement and the problems in the process of application. As a consequence, the subjects of response obligations are generally the initiating organ or their subordinate organs. In the ex-post evaluation system, the evaluation intends to provide a retrospective evaluation of the effectiveness of the existing laws and regulations. The content of the evaluation often involves problems in the laws themselves, problems in the law enforcement process, and problems existing in the application of laws, so the subjects of response obligations involve the legislative, judicial, and administrative organs depending on the content of the evaluation.

(2) Content and methods for perfecting the mechanism of response to the evaluation of the SEZ's legislation.

According to the practical experience of the work of the evaluation of Shenzhen's legislation, in the past the responses to the evaluation of the legislation are often carried out in the "report" manner.[12] This approach has the following three major drawbacks. First, the content of the report is random and cannot fully reflect problems presented in the conclusions of the evaluation. Second, the subjects of response rights do not review the content of the report, thus leading to a lack of oversight of the response content. Third, the city has not established the mechanism for publicizing and monitoring the follow-up work of the measures promised by the report, and the report might become formalistic. Thus, the mechanism of response to the evaluation of SEZ's legislation should be perfected in the following aspects.

First of all, the responses to the "enaction, amendment and abolition" of laws and regulations. The legislative bodies should respond to the suggestions for "enaction, amendment and abolition" of the SEZ regulations in the conclusions of the evaluation. In response to the results of such evaluations, it is recommended that the SEZ should establish a "conversion mechanism from the legislation evaluation

---

[12]After Shenzhen evaluates the *School Safety Management Regulations of Shenzhen*, Lin Yuanchang, the Director of the Education, Science, Culture and Health Commission of the Standing Committee of the Municipal People's Congress responded to the conclusions of the evaluation in the form of a report. See Lin Yuanchang, "Report on the Implementation of the School Safety Management Regulations of Shenzhen", on the 10th Meeting of the Standing Committee of the 4th Session of the Shenzhen Municipal People's Congress on January 18, 2007. http://baike.baidu.com/view/3324062.htm.

report to the legislative proposals".[13] The organizers of the evaluation of the SEZ legislation should promptly send the conclusions of the evaluation to the law-making organs, which should carefully study and review the evaluation report, understand the defects in the enforcement process of the regulations and the feasibility of the evaluation suggestions, and write the response report. For the problems presented in the conclusions of the evaluation, the organs with the obligation to respond to the evaluation should respond positively: for feasible suggestions in the results of the evaluation, relevant authorities should formulate legislative proposals based on the results of the evaluation and make decisions on "enaction, amendment and abolition"; regarding the suggestions not adopted, a detailed statement and explanation should be provided.

Second, the responses to issues such as law enforcement and application. Such issues are generally responded to by relevant administrative and judicial organs. Because there is not necessarily an affiliation between subjects involved in the response to the evaluation (subjects of response rights and subjects of response obligations),[14] it is special to deal with such evaluation responses. First of all, Shenzhen should establish a system of communication and exchange among various organs and departments. For issues among organs and departments with power affiliation, the evaluation organizer should deliver the evaluation report to relevant departments and request the organs with response obligation to give a response and urge them to correct the problems and make improvements; regarding issues among organs and departments without power affiliation, the evaluation organizer should deliver the evaluation report to their common superior organ and urge them to respond to the problems reflected in the conclusions of the evaluation. After receiving the evaluation response report from the organs with response obligation, the competent authority should organize certain staff to review the content of the response and decide on approval or disapproval. With regard to the disapproved evaluation response report, the competent authority may request the organs with response obligation to continue improving the response report according to the conclusions of the evaluation and submit the response report again until it is approved. And then, the evaluation response report should be published on the relevant website for the convenience of public overview. Regarding the writing of the response report, the subjects of response to the evaluation should refer to the conclusions of the evaluation, combine the actual situations of the Shenzhen Special Economic Zone, include the valuable problems reflected in the evaluation results on the agenda and resolve them promptly. With each problem as a basic listed item, the organs should propose the budget, time, plan and effects for solving such problems in detail in the evaluation response report. The organs with response obligation should reevaluate the evaluation response plan at a

---

[13]See Wang Quansheng, Chen Guang, "Analysis of Response Delay after the Post-Legislation Evaluation", *Theory and Reform*, 2008(05).

[14]This mainly exists between administrative organs and judicial organs. If the Municipal Government of Shenzhen evaluates the regulations it has enacted and the evaluation results reflect some problems in the process of applying the law by judicial organs, then the Municipal Government of Shenzhen should not directly require the judicial organs to give a response, but the Municipal People's Congress of Shenzhen should serve as the subject of response right.

specific time and report the effects of the implementation of the response plan to the competent authorities, thus forming a circle management system of "(ex-ante) evaluation—legislation—(ex-post) evaluation—improvement—evaluation". Finally, the subjects of response to the evaluation should promptly disclose the implementation of the evaluation response plan to the public through the website and Weibo, so as to strengthen internal and external oversights and achieve a virtuous circle of the system of evaluation of legislation.

Song Ming Associate Professor at the Law School of Shenzhen University, Ph.D., with research interests in: Administrative Law, Procedural Law and Sociology of Law; Chen Jialin, Master Student at the Law School of Shenzhen University, with research interests in: Administrative Law.

Chapter 6
Building up the Sino-African Relationship of Cooperation on Sustainable Development

H. E. Hailemeskel Tefera

Abstract The African Minister, H. E. Hailemeskel Tefera, made a conclusion on the major standpoint of the seminar, which is jointly sponsored by IPRCC and UNDP and was undertaken by the China Center for Special Economic Zone Research at Shenzhen University, the successful measure of the development of Chinese poverty reductions and the principles that could be learnt and taken as best practice for Africa. It has also been pointed out that this seminar contributed to the Sino-African relationship of cooperation on sustainable development, which is of great benefit to both sides.

Keywords Industrial restructuring · Industry upgrading · Optimization of the industrial structure

China-Africa Poverty Reduction and Development Seminar-the Development of SEZs in China and Poverty Reduction, which was jointly hosted by IPRCC and UNDP, and was undertaken by the China Center for Special Economic Zone Research at Shenzhen University, was convoked from January 9th to 13th, 2012 in Shenzhen. The main purpose of the seminar was probing into how African countries accelerate their economic and social development, reducing poverty and implementing the progress of Millennium Development Goals by referencing the experience of China's economic development and investment policy. China and African countries will share extensive and in-depth experiences in policy, systems, public-private partnerships and technical issues. The implementation of special economic zones, industrial development from planning and design to management and operation, as well as the experience of attracting private investments in the regulatory and corporate environment provide the main materials for the discussion. The African Minister, H. E. Hailemeskel Tefera, summarized the basic lessons of the seminar on the building of the Sino-African relationship of cooperation on sustainable development.

H. E. Hailemeskel Tefera (✉)
Ministry of Urban Development & Construction of Ethiopia, Addis Ababa, Ethiopia
e-mail: sez@szu.edu.cn

© Social Sciences Academic Press 2020
Y. Yuan (ed.), *Studies on China's Special Economic Zones 3*,
Research Series on the Chinese Dream and China's Development Path,
https://doi.org/10.1007/978-981-13-9841-4_6

1 Under the Development of the Government Strategies for China's SEZs and the Framework for the Macro Economic Policy

Africans take the responsibility to craft the suitable policy that assures the rapid development of their countries learning broadly from the developmental trends of the SEZs (Special Economic Zones) in China. Moreover, creating a favorable environment that could attract and suit those domestic and overseas entrepreneurs and achieving a sustainable and continuous growth of development has to be given important attention. The experience of the SEZs is very promising and helpful in addressing the demand for fast developmental need of Africa. China had implemented the reform and opening-up policy some 30 years ago, and this policy highly helped China in solving poverty and unemployment.

The achievement of the rapid economic growth of China is the result of institutional transformation including comprehensive reform of the planned economy and the construction of a market economy. As a matter of this fact, today, China is enjoying the fruits of the appropriate policy that emanated from local thought and was best suited to the social, cultural, political and economic context.

It has generally been accepted that economic development and poverty reduction are correlated. Therefore, Africans have great responsibilities in providing the poor with the opportunities for livelihood by making use of the labor that they have by employing a labor-intensive developmental model. Human capital has to be built up by the provision of social infrastructures. In the long run, it is this capacity that increases the level of income of the people. In today's scenario, African government leaders are committed to assuring the development of their nation in particular and of the continent in general. This historical time is very helpful to Africa's development and prosperity by learning from China. The connection already established in cooperation between Africa and China is becoming a good framework in creating a favorable environment for mutual benefit.

As the practice of the Special Economic Zone of Shenzhen shows the world, the whole evolution of those industries some 30 years back required hard work, the best plan and leadership commitment to transform into current high-tech industries. The key roles that the government plays in supporting and making policy, providing basic infrastructures and finances are the core areas that enable the entrepreneurs to get on the track of playing their roles and responsibilities.

2 Six Main Principles That Could Be Learnt and Taken as Best Practice for Africa

2.1 Implementing the Principle of Agricultural Development-Led Industrialization

For those African nations, which are agrarian countries, the building up of industry can be realized only through the implementation of a strategy of agricultural and rural centered economic and industrial development. It must be underlined that the implementation of agricultural development-led industrialization would at the same time mean that fostering the expansion of the growth of industry side by side to the agricultural development. Thus, it is true that the general economic development of the country as well as the pace of the growth of the industrial sector is determined by the development of the agricultural sector. Fast industrial development can only be secured when the industrial sector could reach the stage of producing various agricultural inputs and consumer goods, and enable to supple agricultural products with added value. If the agricultural development-led industrialization strategy can be successfully practiced, the developmental strategy would be gradually transformed into an industrial-led developmental strategy.

2.2 Implementing the Principle of Export-Led Industrialization

The foreign market plays a crucial role in securing a dependable market for value added agricultural products, the pace and the direction of the growth of the industrial sector is also determined by the successful implementation of this achievement. On this connection, to encourage the investors' competitiveness on the world market, available information with regard to the type of products, price and timely supply of the products in the required area should be availed lo them. The industrial competitive capacity would be achieved only when it is possible to promote strong export-oriented industry and be able to transform to and implement this industrial competitiveness in other industrial sectors as well.

In fact, the presence of skilled managerial personnel, active involvement of the workers and other factors also contribute to the formation of competitiveness. The development of industrial areas provides fertile soil for the development of many other industries.

2.3 Focusing on the Expansion of a Labor-Intensive Industrial Direction

Abundant and hardworking labor forces are the basis of the competitiveness of African companies. Industries in Africa may have the opportunity of becoming competitive by utilizing this abundant and hardworking force. Unless this force is promoted into productive citizens, the presence of an abundant labor force alone could not be served as a means of reaching the desired good. Conducting strong manpower development is essential to being competitive on the global labor market.

2.4 Implementing an Effective Method of a Domestic-Foreign Investment Partnership

It is known that foreign investors mostly have huge capital and strong world market network coverage. Thus, in Africa where there is a scarcity of investment capital and market access, the inflow of foreign investment to the continent has an important contribution in the promotion of the industrial developmental strategy by way of transferring advanced technology, acquiring a modern management system, activating the investment capital and helping to successfully penetrate the global market.

It is only possible to attract foreign investors by creating a conducive environment that encourages the production of competitive goods both in quality and price, and gives a guarantee to the protection of private property. Thus, the private sector is said to be an engine of the industrial developmental strategy, when a fertile ground that boosts the capacity of the industrial developmental strategy can be formulated by making the private sector become the prime move of the strategy for industrial development and the wide participation of foreign investors in partnerships with the domestic ones.

2.5 Implementing the Direction Where the Government Will Play a Leading Managerial Role

One thing noted in the seminar is that the government should not intervene in the investment areas where the private sector can successfully be involved. Thus, the governments of Africa have to limit themselves in the identification of problems lo be posed in connection with market failure and find ways of solving the constraints based on its execution and financial capacity and appropriate experience gained from those countries which successfully complemented industrial development.

In its short intervention, the government is to play a role in designing a system that helps fill the market failure gap and in its long-term plan, it should be involved in face-lifting the mechanisms that encourage the private entrepreneurs to fill the market failure gap by themselves. In short, the role of the government in industrial development should focus on the formulation of favorable conditions for the development of the private sector and be involved in the activities where the private sector is unable to participate.

2.6 Creating Favorable Conditions for Industrial Development and Developmental Entrepreneurs

In order to enable the developmental entrepreneurs to serve as an engine of industrial development, a better enabling environment for the development of the private sector has to be facilitated by way of creating macro-economic stability, modernizing the financial system, creating dependable physical infrastructure services, developing effective human resources and creating an efficient civil service and judiciary system that supports development.

Finally, Africans learn from the Chinese model how to create a stable macro-economic system by getting rid of the rent-seeking trend to promote and strengthen efforts of the developmental entrepreneurs. To help the developmental entrepreneurs work and be directed in a meaningful plan and become involved in investments in the long run, the creation of a stable and foreseeable economic environment is necessary. However, healthy economic growth has a decisive role to play in the promotion of macro-economic stability; the policies formulated by the government could also be conducive to supporting the accomplishment of this objective as seen from Chinese experience. To this effect, the creation of a modernized financial system suitable for development is a compulsory instrument.

3 Conclusions and Policy Suggestions

In conclusion, with great honor, the minister of Africa thanks IPRCC, LGOP, all the members of the staff of Shenzhen University, moderators, presenters and UNDP for making this seminar happen. This seminar provides entrepreneurs with a platform to obtain information on African investments, showing some challenges that Chinese companies are facing. Moreover, it is a great opportunity for the CEOs of Huawei, ZTE and Tencent companies as well as the whole management department to give an eloquent welcome and a brief introduction to the minister.

Chapter 7
Dynamic Game Analysis of Technology Diffusion and Innovation Performance: Case Study of China's Automotive Industry

Shenglan Li, Yun Zhang and Rui Feng

Abstract Automobile groups in China have two survival modes: joint venture with multinational corporations or independent development. Based on the three-stage dynamic game model, this paper studies the relationship between the technology diffusion from the transnational automobile group in the process of joint venture and the technology innovation and the R&D strategies of Chinese and foreign sides, as well as how technology diffusion can influence the competition between domestic brands and joint venture brands and the development of domestic enterprises independent innovation? The model reveals the delicate relationship between technology diffusion, innovation performance and technology development of the automotive industry. The conclusions drawn can be well supported by what is happening in the real world, they can develop and supplement the research of international technology diffusion and provide reference for the formulation of automotive industry policies and the developmental strategies of automobile enterprises.

Keywords Automotive industry · R&D · Technology diffusion · Innovation performance · Game

1 Introduction

The technology diffusion effects of international R&D refer to the improvements of the level of technology and productivity in the host country through involuntary technology spillovers and by international trade, foreign direct investment (FDI) and independent innovation (Wolfgang 2004). The "market-for-technology" strategy has been implemented by the Chinese government in the automotive industry since the early 1980s for the purposes of realizing the transfer of domestic technology by attracting direct investments from multinational automobile giants and promoting technological progress and economic development. On the one hand, a series of joint ventures and cooperative enterprises with foreign investors have

S. Li (✉) · Y. Zhang · R. Feng
Lingnan College, Sun Yat-Sen University, Guangzhou 510275, China
e-mail: lnslsl@mail.sysu.edu.cn

© Social Sciences Academic Press 2020
Y. Yuan (ed.), *Studies on China's Special Economic Zones 3*,
Research Series on the Chinese Dream and China's Development Path,
https://doi.org/10.1007/978-981-13-9841-4_7

rapidly improved the overall level of the production technologies of China's automotive industry through the CKD[1] model, leading to a leap-forward development of its scale and output value. By 2009, China had become the world's largest producer and consumer of vehicles. On the other hand, the CKD model fails to fully build up the capability of independent innovation of local auto enterprises, which show the following characteristics. First, under the triple pressure of a lack of funds, backward technology and industrial policies, local enterprises are increasingly dependent on multinational corporations. Second, local enterprises perform badly in imitation and assimilation because multinational automobile groups exercise a firm control over key technologies and technology innovations. Third, imported vehicles and products of joint ventures basically monopolize the mid-to-high-end auto markets, and local enterprises become gradually competitive in independent production and R&D on the middle and low-end markets.

This paper makes an analysis based on a large number of observations of the reality. According to the ways by which foreign automobile groups enter the Chinese market, they are divided into two categories: export and joint venture. By comparison, it can be found that the joint venture is the dominant strategy. In the latter case, a three-stage dynamic game model has been established to explore the subtle relationship between technology diffusion, innovation performance and technology R&D in the automotive industry. In order to highlight the characteristics of the CKD model, the game players are distinguished in the three different stages of negotiation, R&D and production competition. That is, the game players in the first two stages of negotiation and R&D are Chinese and foreign automobile groups, and domestic enterprises and joint ventures are the game players in the final stage. The domestic enterprises are the subsidiaries of Chinese automobile groups and the joint ventures are held by both Chinese and foreign automobile groups. The paper attempts to answer the three questions: How does the technology diffusion of transnational automobile groups influence the R&D strategies of the Chinese and foreign sides in the process of a joint venture? How does it influence the competition of domestic brands and joint venture brands on the Chinese auto market? How can local enterprises improve self-learning and imitation abilities and find breakthroughs in R&D and independent innovation?

The following sections are organized as follows: The second section presents a review of the literature; the third section introduces the dynamic game model of technology diffusion and innovation performance, and five points are concluded through analysis; the fourth section will use some facts and cases to support the conclusions of the model; and finally, the last section summarizes and proposes relevant policy suggestions.

---

[1]Completely Knocked Down, which means domestic assembly of foreign parts.

2 Review of the Literature

2.1 Approaches of Technology Diffusion

Under the significant influence of technology diffusion, the mechanism of diffusion becomes very important. In the past half a century, related studies reported three approaches for diffusion of technologies: international trade, foreign direct investment and independent innovation (Wolfgang 2004). First, in the production of final products, indirect learning and the use of the high technology contained in foreign semi-finished products through international trade was a good process for technology diffusion (Rivera-Batiz and Romer 1991; Grossman and Helpman 1991; Eaton and Kortum 2002). Through an empirical analysis of the quotations of Swiss patent applications and foreign invention patents, Frederic Sjoholm (1996) found that Swiss firms' patent applications and imports were positively correlated, which meant that importations were conducive to international technology diffusion. Also, this was confirmed by the cases of many East Asian countries that achieved trade success through the "export-learn-export" effects in the 1960s (Rhee et al. 1984).

Second, the most important approach for technology diffusion was FDI (Aitken and Harrison 1999). From the perspective of foreign research, Griffith et al. (2003) studied foreign-owned subsidiaries in the UK and concluded that FDI was important for technology diffusion, which was supported by the research of Keller and Yeaple (2003). Moreover, Markusen (2002) pointed out that the sharing of certain technologies between multinational parent companies and subsidiaries was conducive to the development of related industries in the places where these companies located. Marin and Bell (2006) investigated the data of industrial enterprises in Argentina from 1992 to 1996 and indicated that new technology development, flow and capital of multinational companies had significant technology diffusion effects on enterprises of the host country. With the increase in FDIs in China, there is more and more research on the technology diffusion effects of inbound FDIs. Qi and Li (2008) studied 28 large and medium-sized manufacturing enterprises in China from 2001 to 2005, and pointed out that through demonstration effects and employee mobility, FDIs had weak positive diffusion effects on knowledge creation and management in China. The research by He (2000) showed that FDIs had obvious diffusion effects on the industrial sectors of various provinces and cities in China, and the higher the level o f economic development, the greater the diffusion effect.

2.2 Technology Diffusion and R&D

Technology diffusion improves the R&D performance of the host country. The studies of Eaton and Kortum (1996, 1999) and Keller (2001b) supported the existence of international technology spillovers and found that international technology diffusion played a key role in OECD countries' technological development, instead of relying on domestic R&D investment. Coe and Helpman (1997) estimated the influence of imports on the transfer of international technology and on the growth of total factor productivity (TFP). R&D investments of trading partners were beneficial for the improvement of their total factor productivity, and such benefits could be strengthened with the enhanced degree of trade openness. Moreover, in the knowledge spillover of the North-South trade, the TFP of developing countries had a significant positive correlation with the R&D of industrial trading countries and import trade of machinery and equipment from industrial countries. In an empirical analysis, Li (1999) used the added values, number of jobs, total investment of fixed tangible capital and R&D expenditure of Japanese manufacturing industries from 1981 to 1994 as the samples, and tested the R&D spillover effects within each industry and those of high, medium and low-tech industries among various industries based on the logarithm of the Cobb-Douglas production function.

Actually, the literature above has the background of developed countries, which cannot feasibly explain the phenomena and problems of the CKD model in the Chinese auto industry, nor reflect its characteristics. Therefore, the paper draws on the experience of the methodology of Cai and Li (2011) to establish a three-stage dynamic game model with the characteristics of the Chinese auto industry. The innovation points of this paper include: First, it distinguishes the game players in the three stages of negotiation, R&D and production decision, and introduces the proportion of shareholding and the fee for technology transfer as the parameters into the model in order to fully embody the characteristics of joint ventures and investigate the relationship of technology diffusion and innovation performance from a realistic point of view. Second, the Cournot model includes the factors of technology diffusion and innovation performance, which indicates the relationship between these factors and the R&D strategies of Chinese and foreign sides. Third, according to the longitudinal analysis of the technical characteristics of the automotive industry, the paper obtains the threshold of the relationship between technology diffusion and innovation performance of R&D, and changes the simple conclusion in the past that technology diffusion is beneficial to the innovation performance of a country or an industry or not. The improvement of the model hypothesis can obtain many conclusions that are different from those of the past, which may demonstrate with facts occurring in the real world and cover many phenomena of the Chinese auto industry in the past 30 years and provide reference for the policy-making of the automotive industry and the developmental strategies of automobile enterprises.

3 Dynamic Game Model of Technology Diffusion and Innovation Performance

There is a Chinese automobile group I and a foreign one (f). Suppose, in the initial stage, both automobile groups conduct R&D and produce automobiles sold in China.

The inverse demand function on the Chinese market is $p = a - q$, where p is the price, a is the market capacity and q is the total output: $q = q_c + q_f$.

Both the Chinese and the foreign automobile groups carry out R&D. On the one hand, R&D can improve the innovation performance and decrease the production costs. Suppose that the initial unit cost is c_0, and the R&D[2] of the Chinese and foreign sides can reduce their unit production costs to $c_c = c_0 - x_c$ and $c_f = c_0 - x_f$ respectively, where $0 \leq x_c \leq x_f \leq c_0$. In order to ensure that the output is positive, the market capacity should be large enough, that is $a > 2c_0$. On the other hand, the R&D cost is not only a function of the R&D input level x, but it also relates to the corporate R&D efficiency. For facilitating the analysis, we have the relative coefficient $\rho = \rho_c/\rho_f > 1$ of the R&D efficiency of Chinese and foreign sides and let $\rho_f = 1$. Then the R&D costs of the Chinese and foreign sides are $TC_c(x_c) = \rho x_c^2/2$ and $TC_f(x_f) = x_f^2/2$.[3] The innovation performance of R&D and the efficiency of R&D do not have an effect, the foreign automobile group has the superior technological advantages over those of the Chinese automobile group. And ρ will not change in the short term.

3.1 Case 1: Foreign Automobile Group Exports I Automobiles to the Chinese Market

The Chinese automobile group produces automobiles by depending on independent innovation, and the foreign automobile group conducts R&D and makes products in their home countries, then exports them to China, and pays the tariff t (≥ 0) to the Chinese government.

In this case, the profit of the Chinese automobile group is:

$$\pi_f^e = (a - q^e - c_c^e)q_c^e - \frac{1}{2}\rho x_c^{e2} \tag{1}$$

The profit of the foreign automobile group is:

$$\pi_f^e = (a - q^e - c_f^e)q_f^e - tq_f^e - \frac{1}{2}x_f^{e2} \tag{2}$$

where,

$$q^e = q_c^e + q_f^e, \quad c_c^e = c_0 - x_c^e, \quad c_f^e = c_0 - x_f^e \tag{3}$$

Sub-game perfect equilibrium exists in the case. That is, both parties choose their input level of R&D in the first stage, and decide their production level in the second

---

[2]R&D of the foreign side mainly refers to the R&D investments that are input on production lines, related equipment and a range of car models that specifically import to the Chinese market.

[3]The greater the p, the higher of R&D costs, the lower the innovation performance.

stage. Then, c_c^e and c_f^e in the Cournot model can be considered as given numbers for the fact that Cournot competition in the second stage happens after the completion of R&D. Consequently, the production levels of both parties in the equilibrium are as follows:

$$q_c^e = \frac{a + c_f^e + t - 2c_c^e}{3}, \quad q_f^e = \frac{a + c_c^e - 2c_f^e - 2t}{3} \tag{4}$$

The total production and the price on the market are:

$$q^e = q_c^e + q_f^e = \frac{2a - c_c^e - c_f^e - t}{3}, \quad p^e = \frac{a + c_c^e + c_f^e + t}{3}$$

The profits of both parties in the equilibrium are:

$$\pi_c^e = \frac{(a + c_f^e + t - 2c_c^e)^2}{9} - \frac{1}{2}\rho x_c^{e^2}, \quad \pi_f^e = \frac{(a + c_c^e - 2c_f^e - 2t)^2}{9} - \frac{1}{2}x_f^{e^2} \tag{5}$$

In the first stage, with the given level of R&D of the counterparts, each automobile group decides the level of R&D investment on their own. Then substitute Eq. (3) into Eq. (5), and the first-order condition indicates the R&D level of each group in equilibrium:

$$x_c^e = \frac{4(a - c_0) - 12t}{8 - 3\rho}, \quad x_f^e = 4(a - c_0) - 8t - \frac{16(a - c_0) - 48t}{8 - 3\rho} \tag{6}$$

From Eq. (6) we have $\frac{\partial x_c^e}{\partial t} = \frac{-12}{8-3\rho}$, $\frac{\partial x_f^e}{\partial t} = \frac{24\rho-23}{8-3\rho}$. For $\rho > \frac{8}{3}$, that is, when the R&D performance of the Chinese side is significantly lower than that of the foreign side, the lower tariff reduces the R&D investment of Chinese enterprises and increases that of the foreign one. Therefore, the Chinese government is in favor of setting a high tariff rate for the high-end automobile market with a huge technical gap between Chinese and foreign enterprises; and for $1 < \rho < \frac{8}{3}$, in other words, when the R&D performance of the Chinese automobile group is slightly lower than that of the foreign one, the decrease in the tariff enables Chinese enterprises to increase R&D investment, yet foreign enterprises to reduce R&D investment, which may explain why the tariff is low on the middle and low-end markets with a slight difference in technological level between Chinese and foreign enterprises. Consequently, we reach the conclusions:

Conclusion l: Before the foreign automobile group enters the Chinese market by joint venture, charging high tariffs on high-end automobiles and low tariffs on ordinary ones is beneficial for the motivation of Chinese enterprises for R&D.

3.2 Case 2: Foreign Automobile Group Enters the Chinese Market by Joint Venture

If the foreign automobile group enters China through FDI, it has to set up a joint venture (j) with a Chinese automobile group because the policies and legislations of China do not permit wholly foreign-owned enterprises or those with a proportion of foreign shares exceeding 50% to enter the industry of producing vehicles and engines. In the first stage, the Chinese and foreign automobile groups begin negotiation and both the proportion of shareholding in the joint venture and technology licensing fees paid by the Chinese side will be decided at the same time. Moreover, the profit of the joint venture will be distributed between the Chinese and foreign sides by the proportion of shareholding. Then suppose that the share proportion held by the Chinese automobile group is α, then the shareholding proportion by the foreign automobile group is $1 - \alpha$, and $0.5 \leq \alpha \leq 1$. Since the core technology of the foreign automobile group is completely confidential to the Chinese side, it is allowed only to use the high-tech equipment. A certain percentage of a technology licensing fee is charged from the sales of each vehicle by the Chinese side. The percentage of technology licensing fee is decided as ε in the negotiation of both parties.

If the negotiation is successful, both parties establish a joint venture to produce automobiles in China instead of importing foreign brands. Therefore, there are two types of enterprises on the Chinese automobile market: one is joint venture jointly held by the Chinese and foreign automobile groups, which uses the technology offered by the foreign automobile group, and its unit production cost is $c_j^f = c_0 - x_f^f$; and the other type is subsidiary 100% controlled by a Chinese automobile group, which is called a domestic brand enterprise (i), which relies on the independent R&D and benefits from the technology spillovers of the foreign side through imitation and learning, and its unit production cost is $c_i^f = c_0 - x_c^f - \beta x_f^f$, where $0 < \beta < 1$ is the coefficient of technology diffusion. If the negotiation fails, case 1 will be kept, and β will not be changed in the short term.

In the second stage, Chinese and foreign automobile groups independently make their R&D investments. Indeed, the joint venture does not carry out R&D but uses the technology from the foreign parent company. In most circumstances, for the conduction of R&D on the platform of the automobile group, the vehicle with various styles and different brands in the same automobile group can employ the same technology. Therefore, the R&D investment is decided by the parent company, not the joint venture or domestic brand enterprise.

In the third stage, the joint venture and the domestic brand enterprise individually decide their output. However, the Chinese automobile group is not able to maximize its profit by coordinating the output of the joint venture and the domestic brand enterprise. As a matter of fact, although both parties hold equally 50% of the shares, the foreign automobile group is dominant in the joint venture due to their advanced technology. In the following sections, the sub-game perfect equilibrium will be deducted through the inverse method:

1. The third stage

Similar to case 1, α, ε have been decided in the first stage and c_j^f, c_i^f in the second stage. Therefore, all of these variables can be considered as given in the third stage. According to the Cournot model, the outputs of the domestic brand enterprise and the joint venture are:

$$q_i^f = \frac{a + c_j^f - 2c_i^f}{3} = \frac{a - c_0 + (2\beta - 1)x_f^f + 2x_c^f}{3}$$

$$q_j^f = \frac{a + c_i^f - 2c_j^f}{3} = \frac{a - c_0 - x_c^f + (2 - \beta)x_f^f}{3} \qquad (7)$$

The total output and price on the market are: $q^f = q_i^f + q_j^f = \frac{2a - c_i^f - c_j^f}{3}$, $p^f = \frac{a + c_i^f + c_j^f}{3}$.

The profits at equilibrium are:

$$\pi_i^f = \frac{(a + c_j^f - 2c_i^f)^2}{9} = \frac{\left[a - c_0 + (2\beta - 1)x_f^f + 2x_c^f\right]^2}{9}$$

$$\pi_j^f = \frac{(a + c_i^f - 2c_j^f)^2}{9} = \frac{\left[a - c_0 - x_c^f + (2 - \beta)x_f^f\right]^2}{9} \qquad (8)$$

We have $\frac{\partial q_j^f}{\partial x_f^f} > 0$, $\frac{\partial q_j^f}{\partial x_c^f} < 0$, $\frac{\partial \pi_j^f}{\partial x_f^f} > 0$, $\frac{\partial \pi_j^f}{\partial x_c^f} < 0$; $\frac{\partial q_i^f}{\partial x_c^f} > 0$, $\frac{\partial \pi_i^f}{\partial x_c^f} > 0$, yet the signs of $\frac{\partial q_i^f}{\partial x_f^f}$ and $\frac{\partial \pi_i^f}{\partial x_f^f}$ depend on the magnitude of β and ρ.

Conclusion 2: Chinese independent innovation increases the output and the average profit of the domestic brand enterprise, but decreases those of the joint venture; R&D of the foreign automobile group raises the output and the average profit of the joint venture, yet has uncertain effects on those of the domestic brand enterprise because of the coefficient of technology diffusion. When $\beta > \frac{1}{2}$, improving R&D by the foreign automobile group can increase the output and the average profit of the domestic brand enterprise.

2. The second stage

In this stage, both the foreign and the Chinese automobile groups can decide their R&D investment respectively as α, ε can be seen as given. The foreign automobile group conducts R&D to maximize its benefits, including the profit from the joint venture plus the technology licensing fee paid by the Chinese side deducting its R&D costs.

$$\max_{x_f^f} \pi_f^f = (1 - \alpha)\pi_j^f + \varepsilon p^f q_j^f - \frac{1}{2}x_f^{f2} = (1 - \alpha + \varepsilon)\pi_j^f + \varepsilon c_j^f q_j^f - \frac{1}{2}x_f^{f2} \qquad (9)$$

The Chinese automobile group conducts R&D to maximize its benefits, including the profit from the joint venture and the total profit from the domestic brand enterprise, deducting the technology licensing fee and its R&D costs.

$$\max_{x_c^f} \pi_c^f = \alpha \pi_j^f + \pi_i^f - \varepsilon p^f q_j^f - \frac{1}{2}\rho x_c^{f^2} = (\alpha - \varepsilon)\pi_j^f + \varepsilon c_j^f q_j^f + \pi_i^f - \frac{1}{2}\rho x_c^{f^2}$$

$$(10)$$

In reality, because both sides usually hold 50% of the shares each. Then let $a = 0.5$; due to $0 < \varepsilon \ll 1, 0 < \beta < 1$, then we have $\varepsilon^2 \to 0$, $\beta^2 \to 0$, $\varepsilon\beta \to 0$. On the basis of the first order conditions, we have:

$$x_f^f = \frac{(2\beta - 1)(4a - 4c_0 - 4a\varepsilon + 14c_0\varepsilon - 3a\rho + 3c_0\rho + 3a\varepsilon\rho - 12c_0\varepsilon\rho)}{23 + 16\beta + 8\varepsilon - 12\rho(2 + \beta + \varepsilon)} \quad (11)$$

$$x_c^f = \frac{-9a + 9c_0 - 8a\varepsilon - 3c_0\varepsilon}{23 + 16\beta + 8\varepsilon - 12\rho(2 + \beta + \varepsilon)} \quad (12)$$

3. The first stage

The Nash equilibrium of the negotiation is given as follows:

$$\max_{\alpha,\varepsilon}(\pi_f^f - \pi_f^e)(\pi_c^f - \pi_c^e)$$

$$\text{s.t.} \quad 0.5 \le \alpha \le 1 \quad (13)$$

where, x_f^f and x_c^f are given by Eqs. (11) and (12).

F.O.C

$$\frac{\partial \pi_f^f}{\partial \varepsilon}(\pi_c^f - \pi_c^e) + \frac{\partial \pi_c^f}{\partial \varepsilon}(\pi_f^f - \pi_f^e) = 0 \quad (14)$$

$$\frac{\partial \pi_f^f}{\partial \alpha}(\pi_c^f - \pi_c^e) + \frac{\partial \pi_c^f}{\partial \alpha}(\pi_f^f - \pi_f^e) = 0$$

The technology licensing fee brings more profit to the foreign side at the cost of depriving the benefits of the Chinese side. Therefore, $\frac{\partial \pi_f^f}{\partial \varepsilon} > 0$, $\frac{\partial \pi_c^f}{\partial \varepsilon} < 0$, and then $\pi_c^f - \pi_c^e > 0$, $\pi_f^f - \pi_f^e > 0$. It can be seen that the joint venture is a dominant strategy, so Chinese and foreign automobile groups seek long-term cooperation.

Because the results are complicated, we do not give the explicit solution of ε. Through comparing the total auto production and profit of case 1 and case 2, the total output and profit are increased after the foreign automobile group enters the Chinese market through a joint venture.

4. Long-term situation

Finally, in the long run, β and ρ may change. According to the practical evidence, we set $a = 50$, $c_0 = 6$, $\alpha = 0.5$, $\varepsilon = 0.03$, then the following graphs are x_f^f and x_c^f

relating to β and ρ respectively (Figs. 1 and 2). By the comparative static analysis, it can be found that the technology diffusion and innovation performance have a significant influence on the R&D strategies of the joint venture and the domestic brand enterprise.

First of all, Fig. 1 shows, when ρ is large, that is, there is a big difference between the innovation performance of the Chinese and foreign sides, x_f^f nearly linearly increases as β increases, which means the foreign automobile group can gain substantial technology transfer or licensing fees through transferring backward technology; when ρ is close to 1, that is, there is little difference between the innovation performance of the Chinese and foreign sides, x_f^f gradually increases for a period

Fig. 1 Three-dimensional graph of x_f^f relating to β and ρ

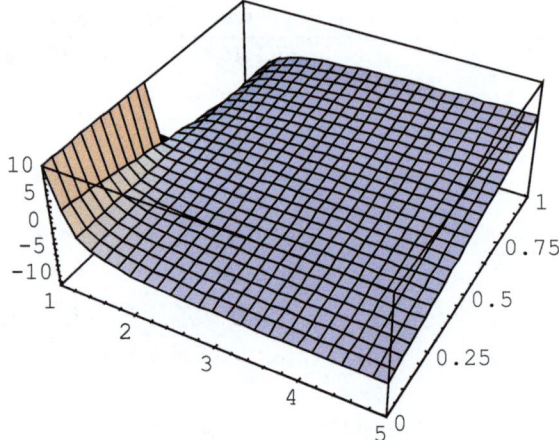

Fig. 2 Three-dimensional graph of x_c^f relating to β and ρ

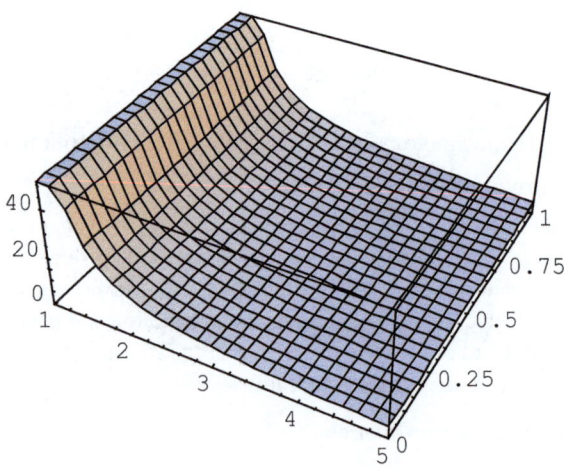

and then suddenly decreases as β increases. Moreover, when the technology diffusion coefficient β exceeds a set value, the foreign automobile group refuses the technology transfer due to the worry of losing its technological advantage.

Second, Fig. 2 indicates that, when ρ is large, the relationship between x_c^f and β becomes U-shaped. In other words, when β is lower than a set value, the technology diffusion does not bring the leap of core technology for the Chinese side; when β exceeds the set value, the technology diffusion is substantially beneficial to the Chinese side, which has an incentive to increasing R&D in the forms of joint design and R&D cooperation and narrowing the gap of technology. However, if ρ is close to 1, the relationship between x_c^f and β becomes an inverse U-shape. That is, when β is smaller than the set value, the Chinese side cannot solely depend on imitating the technology of the foreign side, but increase R&D investment and compete with the joint venture by independent innovation; when β exceeds the set value, the Chinese side relies on the benefit of technology diffusion, with no incentives to increase R&D investment.

Therefore, we have:

Conclusion 3: In the market area with a big difference of innovation performance between the Chinese and the foreign sides, when the coefficient of technology diffusion is smaller than a set value, the R&D investment of the Chinese side decreases with the increasing technology diffusion, with no R&D investment from the foreign side towards the Chinese side; however, when the coefficient exceeds the set value, the technology diffusion has positive effects on the R&D investment of both the Chinese and the foreign automobile groups.

Conclusion 4: In the market area with a small difference of innovation performance between the Chinese and foreign sides, technology diffusion should be controlled within a certain scope lower than the set value, which can promote the R&D investment of both the Chinese and the foreign automobile groups.

4 Conclusions and Suggestions

According to a three-stage dynamic game model, the paper reaches a series of conclusions that are not only supported by the facts of the development of the Chinese automobile industry, but it also explains the dynamic relationship between technology diffusion and innovation performance and their influence on the R&D strategies of Chinese and foreign automobile groups cooperating with the CKD model, thus profoundly influencing the growth of independent innovation enterprises and the whole automobile industry in China. Indeed, on the low-end automobile market with little difference in innovation performance, multinational corporations are inclined to take the approach of a joint venture, which leads to the fierce competition of domestic enterprises and the joint venture on the auto market of A-class and B-class. Undoubtedly in a short period of time, due to the technology diffusion, the R&D investment of the foreign automobile group not only increases the output and profit of the joint venture but also improves those of domestic brand enterprises. Both sides of the joint venture are in favor of long-term cooperation due to huge benefits, especially in that China has rapidly become the largest auto production country by the CKD model. However, in the long run, the strategy of market for technology can-not realize the assimilation and absorption of advanced technologies and even independent development will be lost in the traps of shrinking capabilities of independent development and design and technology dependency. Aiming at the ultimate goals of independent design and domestic brands, and competition with international auto giants, the new energy and new-tech vehicles without a big difference in innovation performance will be the last opportunity of Chinese enterprises.

Regarding how to promote the R&D investment and technological advancement of Chinese automobile enterprises, considering the model conclusions and the reality, we propose the following policy suggestions for enterprises and the government:

First, Chinese automobile enterprises should focus on the development of vehicles by means of CKD instead of solely "follow-suit", improve the innovation performance through technological conversion and innovation efficiency, enhance the assimilation and absorption of introduced technologies, realize the joint design by narrowing the technology gap, and finally achieve independent design, get rid of technology reliance and build domestic brands. Moreover, they should learn the advanced experience of management and marketing of the foreign side and establish the regulated modern corporate system in order to strengthen their competitive power. Also, they should enhance mergers and restructuring and achieve a larger scale and professionalism by low-cost expansion.

Second, the Chinese government should require strict contract performance and have necessary regulations on the transfer of some core technologies from the foreign side to the Chinese side as stipulated in the joint venture contract, which cannot be fulfilled due to the dominant role of the foreign side. Moreover, the administrative restrictions on the complete vehicle production should be loosened. In other words, the government should "open up to the outside world" and "also to the domestic enterprises", encourage private enterprises to enter the automotive industry, reduce the threshold of automobile investment projects and form a perfectly competitive market. Importantly, in view of the last opportunity in new energy and new tech vehicles, the Chinese government should formulate policies of positively supporting the new energy vehicle industry, increase subsidies or fund supports for fundamental and long-term research projects, make policies and rules on the construction of facilities for the buying, charging, parking, traveling and charging of electric vehicles and hybrid power vehicles, accelerate the construction of supporting service facilities, such as vehicle recharging, maintenance and repair, and battery management in communities and perfect the developmental environment for new energy vehicles.

References

Aitken, Brian and Ann Harrison. "Do Domestic Firms Benefit from Foreign Direct Investment? Evidence from Venezuela," Amer Econ. Rev. 1999, 89:3, pp. 605–18.

Coe, D. E, E. Helpman, and A. Hoffmaister. North- South R&D Spillovers [J]. Economic Journal, 1997, (107): 134–149.

Dapeng Cai and Jie Li, Quid pro quo and the enforcement of intellectual property rights protection: a bargaining approach [J], The Journal of International Trade&Economic Development, 2011, pp:1–18.

Eaton, Jonathan; Eva Gutierrez and Samuel Kortum. "Technology, Geography, and Trade," Econometrica 2002, 70:5, pp. 1741–79.

Eaton, J and S Kortum. Trade in Ideas: Patenting and Productivity in the OECD [J]. Journal of International Economics, 1996, (40): 251–278.

Eaton, J and S Kortum. International Patenting and Technology Diffusion: Theory and Measurement [J]. International Economic Review, 1999, (40): 537–570.

Grossman, Gene and Elhanan Helpman. Innovation and Growth in the World Economy, Cambridge, MA: MIT Press. 1991.

He Jie, Further Accurate Quantification of the Spillover Effects of Foreign Direct Investment on China's Industrial Sector, The Journal of World Economy, 2000(12), pp. 29–36.

James R. Markusen, Keith E. Maskus. Discriminating Among Alternative Theories of the Multinational Enterprise, Review of international Economics, 2002, Volume 10, Issue 4, pages 694–707.

Keller W. Geographic Localization of International Technology Diffusion [J]. American Economic Review, 2001b, (92): 120–142.

Keller, Wolfgang and Stephen Yeaple. "Multinational Enterprises, International Trade, and Productivity Growth: Firm Level Evidence from the United States," IMF work. 2003. Pap. 248.

Li Ping, Analysis of Spillover Effects in Technology diffusion, Nankai Journal (Philosophy, Literature and Social Science Edition), 1999(8), pp. 28–33.

MARIN A, BELL M. Technology spillovers from foreign direct investment(FDI): the active role of MNC subsidiaries in Argentina in the 1990s[J]. Journal of Development Studies, 2006, 42(4): 678–697.

QI J, LI H. Spillover effect of FDI on China knowledge creation[J]. Chinese Management Studies, 2008, 2(2): 86–96.

Rachel Griffith, Stephen Redding, and Helen Simpson. Foreign Ownership and Productivity: New Evidence from the Service Sector and the R&D Lab Oxford[J]. Review of Economic Policy, 2003, Volume20, Issue3, Pp. 440–456.

Rivera-Batiz, Luis and Paul Romer. "Economic Integration and Endogenous Growth," Quart. J. Econ. 1991.106:2, pp. 531–55.

Wolfgang Keller. "International Technology Diffusion", Journal of Economic Literature, 2004, Vol. 42, No. 3(Sep., 2004), pp. 752–782.

Yung-Whee Rhee, Bruce Ross-Larson, and Garry Pursell, Korea's competitive edge: Managing the entry into world markets, 1984, p 163, Published for the World Bank [by] the Johns Hopkins University Press (Baltimore, Md.).

Li Shenglan Deputy Dean of Lingnan College, Sun Yat-Sen University, Professor, with research interests in: Western economics, regional economics, industrial economics; Zhang Yun, Feng Rui, Ph.D. of Lingnan College, SunYat-Sen University. Key research project "Empirical Research of Legal System and China's Economic Growth" supported by the National Social Science Fund of China (project no. 08AJL004).

Chapter 8
An Industrial Transformation Path Across the Middle Income Trap

Zhongxiong Cao

Abstract In the history of the development of the world economy, countries such as Japan and South Korea have successfully achieved a leap to high-income economies through a series of industrial transformations at the middle-income level, while Latin American countries are mired in the so-called "middle income trap". How to become a high-income economy by avoiding the middle income trap is one of the biggest challenges faced by the Chinese economy. Exploring the root causes of the "middle income trap" and the law of leap-forward development can help China accelerate its transformation of the economic development model and achieve sustainable development. From the perspective of industrial transformation and development, this paper compares the successful cases of Japan and South Korea, analyzes typical Latin American and Southeast Asian countries that have stumbled into the "middle income trap", investigates the logical relationship between the "middle income trap" and industrial division of labor and international industrial transfer, summarizes the international experience, and puts forward countermeasures and suggestions for China's transformation and development.

Keywords Middle income trap · Industrial transformation · Innovation

1 Introduction

In the history of the development of the world economy, countries such as Japan and South Korea have successfully leaped forward to high-income economies through a series of reforms during the upper middle-income stage, while the industrial transformation and upgrading of Latin American countries stalled with serious contrasts and problems of slow growth, structural issues and unfair income distribution and they were mired in the so-called "middle income trap". In 2011, China's per capita GDP reached US$5445/person and joined the middle-income economies. How to become a high-income economy by avoiding the middle-income trap is one of the

Z. Cao (✉)
China Development Institute, Shenzhen 518000, China
e-mail: caozx@cdi.com.cn

© Social Sciences Academic Press 2020
Y. Yuan (ed.), *Studies on China's Special Economic Zones 3*,
Research Series on the Chinese Dream and China's Development Path,
https://doi.org/10.1007/978-981-13-9841-4_8

biggest challenges faced by the Chinese economy. Exploring the root causes of the "middle income trap" and the law of leap-forward development can help China accelerate its transformation of the economic development model and achieve sustainable development. From the perspective of the "middle income trap", this paper attempts to elaborate on the view that the middle income trap is essentially a trap of the low degree of industrialization, and the transformation of economic developmental strategies and the changes of the industrial path are necessary conditions to avoid the "middle income trap".

2   Background of Economic Transformation and the Middle Income Trap

(I)   Conceptual analysis of the middle income trap

The middle-income stage is a unique stage in the whole growth process, a key point in the development of industrial transformation, and an important turning point in development for some economies. The concept of the "middle income trap" was first proposed by the World Bank's *EAST ASIAN VISIONS: Perspectives on Economic Development* in 2006, which clearly defined it as "the strategies for the growth from low-income economies to middle-income economies which cannot be repeated for their climbing to high-income economies, further economic growth is locked by the original growth mechanism, it is difficult for the national income per capita to exceed the upper limit of US$10,000 and a country may easily enter the stagnation period of economic growth". In 2010, in the report of "Robust Recovery, Rising Risk", the "middle income trap" was further elaborated as: "For decades, many economies in Latin America and the Middle East have been stuck in this middle income trap, where countries are struggling to remain competitive as high-volume, low-cost producers in the face of rising wage costs, but are yet unable to move up the value chain and break into fast-growing markets for knowledge and innovation-based products and services". From the perspective of the process of post-war world economic development, only a few countries and regions, such as Japan and the "Four Asian Tigers", have successfully proceeded from middle-income economies to high-income economies. Although the economic development of most developing countries has experienced ups and downs, they remain in the middle-income stage for long and cannot become high-income economies. From the World Bank's understanding of this concept, the so-called "middle income trap" aims at late-developing countries, especially those in the developmental stage, whose fundamental problem is development and transformation. These middle-income countries maintain their original developmental paths and industrial choices for a long time. Their industrial structure has not been transformed and the developmental model has not been changed. As a result, their economic development is stagnated or even seriously deteriorated (Table 1).

Table 1 Distribution of GDP per capita of the economies according to the statistics of World Bank and IMF in 2011

		Low income	Middle income		High income
			Lower middle-income	Upper middle-income	
		$1005 or less	$1006–$3975	$3976–$12,275	$12,276 or more
Number of economies	IMF	32	50	46	56
	World Bank	33	50	49	71
Peak/valley GDP per capita	Peak	903	3965	11,170	113,533
	Valley	216	1062	3992	12,671
	Global average	10,144			
World Bank	Highest	935	3798	11,711	172,676
	Lowest	139	1075	4030	12,580
	Global average	10,034			

Note (1) 184 economies of the IMF data by GDP; (2) 203 economies of the World Bank data, and some data were collected during the years before 2011; (3) Unit: US dollars/person

According to the World Bank's latest 2011 standards: the economies are divided into the following groups according to the calculated GDP per capita: there are 32 low-income economies ($1005 or less); 50 lower middle-income economies ($1006–$3975); 46 upper middle-income economies ($3976–$12,275) and 56 high-income economies ($12,276 or more). According to these standards, the per capita GDP of the International Monetary Fund (IMF) is classified as 33 low-income economies; 50 lower middle-income economies; 49 upper middle-income economies; and 71 high-income economies. In terms of the global average, 43% of economies are below the middle income, and the world is still at the lower middle-income level and at a critical stage of surpassing the middle income.

(II) **Judgment of China's risk of "middle income trap"**

In 2011, when the per capita GDP reached US$5445/person (according to the World Bank data), China became an upper middle-income economy. In particular, Guangdong's per capita GDP had already reached US$7977/person. The issue of whether China is in the middle income trap is a hot topic in academic debates. At the press conference of the *2011 China Economic Growth Report*, Liu Wei claimed that China is now entering the middle-income developmental stage and there is a possibility of falling into the "middle income trap", so we should be alert. Zhang Qizai from the Chinese Academy of Social Sciences indicated that although China's overall competitiveness was generally strong, there were indeed structural defects, which would be a serious challenge for China to fall into the "middle income trap". However, Xue (2010) pointed out that China was indeed facing the challenge of "expectation management", macroeconomic regulation and various social problems, but he was optimistic that it was not necessary to worry too much about the threat of the "middle income trap". Hu (2011) warned that China should not devise a "middle income trap".

In this paper, it is believed that China's current per capita income has reached the level of middle-income countries and we are facing a key turning point. How to avoid falling into the "middle income trap" is undoubtedly an important challenge for China. According to the purchasing power parity (PPP) and eliminating the price factor, China's current per capita income level is only comparable to Japan's in the mid-1970s and South Korea's in the early 1990s. The Chinese economy has many problems, such as excessive reliance on exports and investment, and prominent structural contrasts of industrial sectors. It has not yet progressed to the stage when the middle and high-tech industries are dominant, and still faces the challenge of the "middle income trap" in the second half of the process of marching towards high-income countries. Judging from the general characteristics of the "middle income trap", China's situation is not special. On the one hand, the traditional comparative advantages gradually disappear, and on the other hand, the new comparative advantages have not yet been revealed. First of all, the difficulty in adjusting China's industrial structure breeds the greatest risk of economic development. China's industries with comparative advantages are mainly based on labor- and resource-intensive export-oriented industries. Second, the relatively slow urbanization process in China has alleviated the severity of urban problems. The urban-rural dual structure has further aggravated the risk of falling into the "middle income trap". In addition, the expansion of the income distribution gap in China is accompanied by an absolute increase in the income of various social groups.

A lot of scholars in China have proposed the basic ideas of avoiding and passing through the middle-income stage by the transformation of the industrial structure. The studies from the perspective of the structural transformation are explained below. Zhang (2011) put forward the idea that the change of model and adjustment of structure are the correct choices to avoid the "middle income trap". Since the beginning of the new century, China has repeatedly proposed the transformation of its developmental model and the adjustment of its structure for the purposes of avoiding the "middle income trap" and maintaining long-term rapid economic growth. Wang (2011) stressed that the economic developmental model must adapt to changes in the developmental environment and developmental stage and avoid the original developmental model. Liu (2011) made an analysis of China's various developmental advantages to avoid the "middle income trap" and thought that with such advantages, China's economic development can avoid and overcome the "middle income trap". Chen (2011) analyzed the transition from comparative advantages to competitive advantages and emphasized the transformation of internal and external developmental methods for successfully avoiding the "middle income trap". Thus, whether China's economic development can smoothly pass through the "middle income trap" and achieve long-term stable and rapid development is in essence the transformation of the economic developmental model and the choice and transformation of the economic developmental strategy.

3   Economic Transformation and Experience and Lessons of the "Middle Income Trap"

During the course of development, there are often two different developmental fates faced with the challenge of the "middle income trap". Both the experience of successful countries and the lessons of economic stagnation and even retrogression of countries caught in the "middle income trap" have attracted the attention of governments and academic circles.

(I)   Successful experience of countries avoiding the "middle income trap"

Historical experience shows that although there are large differences among countries, there is a fundamental consistency between the structural transition point of economic growth and the per capita GDP level. In the 1960s and 1970s, European and American developed countries and Latin American and East Asian countries achieved breakthroughs in per capita GDP of US$4000 in the similar stages. Japan, South Korea and the developed countries in Europe and America successfully crossed this "watershed", vigorously adjusted their industrial structure, developed the heavy industry, implemented the export substitution strategy, successfully achieved transformation from labor-intensive to technology-intensive, generally maintained a high-speed economic growth for more than 10 years and realized the breakthrough of US$10,000 per capita (Table 2).

Japan's per capita GDP was US$4281 in 1974 and reached US$16,882 in 1986. South Korea's per capita GDP broke through the second time point in 1988, reaching US$4466, and US$12,249 in 1996. For the transition from upper middle-income to

Table 2   Time points of developed economies avoiding the "middle income trap"

Economies	Middle income					High income		2011
	Lower		Upper					
	Year	GDP per capita	Year	GDP per capita		Year	GDP per capita	GDP per capita
European Union	1962	1054	1975	4231		1988	12,335	34,848
OECD members	1960	1334	1974	4349		1987	13,136	37,029
Japan	1966	1059	1974	4281		1986	16,882	45,903
South Korea	1977	1071	1988	4466		1996	12,249	22,424
Singapore	1973	1071	1980	4913		1991	13,737	46,241
Hong Kong SAR, China	1971	1102	1979	4563		1990	13,478	34,457

Note The data are sourced from the open data of the World Bank. The GDP of all of the economies are calculated as per the current US dollars

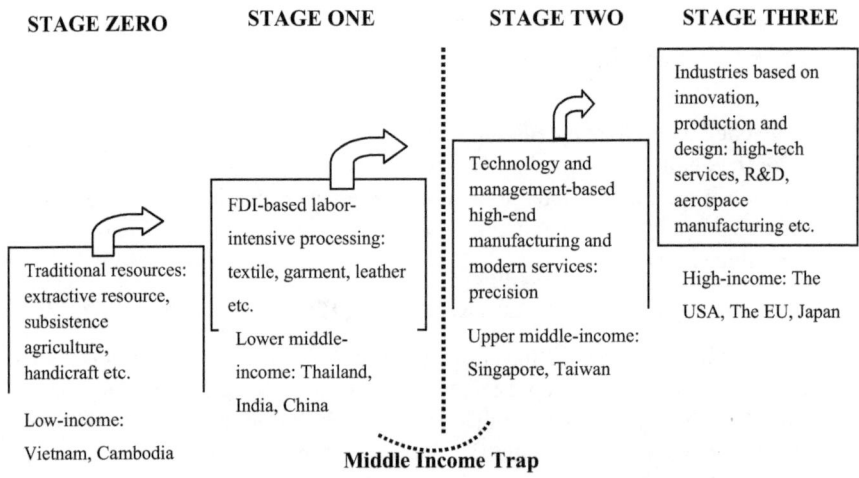

Fig. 1 Industrial transformation and upgrading and the middle income trap

high-income countries, the EU countries took 13 years, the OECD members spent 13 years on average, Japan took about 12 years, South Korea spent 8 years, Singapore took 11 years and Hong Kong spent 11 years (Fig. 1).

Japanese economist Ohno (2009) attributed the cause of the middle income trap to the issue of upgrading the industrial structure. He indicated that a country's economic development had to go through four stages. (1) Stage zero. Economic growth relies heavily on extractive resources, monoculture exports, subsistence agriculture, and simple manufacturing that is not large. (2) Stage one. In this stage, a sufficient mass of manufacturing FDI firms arrive that carry out simple assembly or processing of light industry products for exportation, such as garments, footwear, and foodstuffs. The design, technology, production and marketing are all directed by foreigners, and key materials and parts are imported. (3) Stage two. In this stage, as FDI accumulates and production expands, the domestic supply of parts and components begins to increase significantly. The enhancement of the capability for intrinsic core creation of the product has contributed to the increase in the number of factories, but key manufacturing is under foreign management. Local wages and income cannot rise very much if all of the important tasks continue to be performed by foreign hands, and such countries are vulnerable to the "middle income trap". As the backward countries gradually reduce foreign dependence, internal value rises dramatically. They have the ability to bring about innovations to production and design, and to form a complete industrial chain and standardize production lines. They can respond to more intense international market competition, and reshape the global industrial landscape, such as South Korea, Singapore and Taiwan. (4) Stage three. Countries in this stage acquire the capability to create new products and lead global market trends, like Japan, the USA and the EU.

In the process of industrial upgrading in various stages, the resistance to upgrading the industrial structure in the middle-income stage is even greater, and it is difficult to successfully break through the obstacles of a "glass ceiling" (Table 3).

(II)   Industrial characteristics of Japan and South Korea

The cotton spinning industry in the 1950s, the petrochemical and vehicle industries developed rapidly after the 1960s, the electronics industry that emerged in the 1980s, and the information technology and biomedical industries since the 1990s play a leading role in the development of the entire world economy.

Japan kept up with the pace of technological advancement in the world by introducing, learning, assimilating and innovating advanced technologies. In the 1950s and 1960s, it realized its own industrial modernization in a short period of time. In the 1970s, it implemented industrial transformation and built the capital-intensive industries. In the 1980s, it gradually turned to the technology-intensive industries. In particular, it strengthened the adjustment of the industrial structure centered on knowledge intensification, and promoted the transition of the industrial structure of heavy and chemical industries to high-tech industries (such as electronic computers, information, new energy, life sciences, aerospace, marine development, new materials, etc.). In June 1994, the Japanese government proposed the national strategy of "technology innovation". In 1995, Japan put forward the *Ideas on the Reform of the Economic Structure for the 21st Century*. In 1999, the "Basic Strategy for

Table 3   Time points of the GDP per capita of economies entering income stages (Unit: US dollars/person)

Economies	Lower middle-income		Upper middle-income		High income	GDP per capita	2011
	Year	GDP per capita	Year	GDP per capita	Year	GDP per capita	GDP per capita
East Asia and the Pacific	1978	1011	1995	4188	–	–	8475
Middle-low income	1995	1136	2011	4021	–	–	4021
Middle-income	1994	1052	2011	4575	–	–	4575
Argentina	1962	1148	1988	3978	–	–	10,941
Brazil	1975	1143	1995	4751	2011	–	12,594
Chile	1971	1097	1992	4083	2011	13,866	13,866
Venezuela	1960	1138	1980	4465	2010	13,658	10,810
China	2001	1042	2010	4431	–	–	5445
Malaysia	1977	1084	1995	4287			9656

Note The data are sourced from the open data of the World Bank

Industrial Technology and Industrial Innovation" was presented to intensify industrial innovation, advance the development of venture enterprises and drive forward the economic development of Japan in the 21st century. In 2012, it proposed the *Rebirth of Japan: A Comprehensive Strategy* to redefine the new industrial development and transformation strategy. In its opinion, not the successful system or policy in the past was needed, but an economic model that faces the world, the future, and sustainable development, and the "creative innovation" constantly updating the industrial structure, so as to adapt to environmental changes, foster new industries and new markets, focus on investing in the three fields: energy conservation and environmental protection, health care, as well as agriculture, forestry and fisheries, and enhance its policy support for SMEs (Table 4).

From the industrial developmental paths of the late-developing countries, we must closely follow the global industrial developmental trends to avoid the "middle income trap", continuously put forward transformation and upgrading and we need to build an industrial system connecting to the global industry by relying on innovation and technology updates.

4   Logical Relationship of Middle Income Trap and International Division of Labor

In the international industrial system, middle-income countries rely on the industrial transfer from the developed countries, and the division of labor is mainly concentrated on the middle and low-end sectors, such as processing and manufacturing. With the rapid transition of the product life cycle, some countries have not established their own industrial system and endogenous industrial ecology, which eventually leads to the "middle income trap". While Japan and South Korea are actively undertaking the transfer of new industries, they increase their independent innovation and R&D systems, actively implement the strategy of industrial developmental transformation and "creative innovation" to maintain the new industrial structure, respond to environmental changes, and foster new industries and new markets.

(I)   **Analysis of the industrial value chain in the middle-income stage**

The "smiling curve" shows that processing and manufacturing is located at the bottom of the value-added curve of the industrial chain, and the profit is relatively weak. If the enterprise wants to obtain more added value, it must extend to both ends (Fig. 2).

The adjustment and transfer of international production are embodied as: the division of labor of the global value chain, the developed countries transfer from production to R&D, design and brand marketing, and the developing countries transfer from downstream (processing and assembly of the terminal) to upstream of production (production of key parts). In a certain industry, the lower middle-income countries are more concentrated on processing and assembly in the field of processing trade, such as Vietnam, India, etc., while the market, raw materials, product R&D and

Table 4 The evolution of the leading industries of the USA, Japan, and South Korea since the 1950s

Country	The USA	Japan	South Korea
1950s	Shift from manufacturing to services: steel, electromechanical, construction, vehicles	In the 1950s, the cotton spinning industry was the leading industry, and the pillar industries included textiles, smelting, coal, low-end manufacturing, and transportation	Traditional agricultural country
1960s		Electricity, vehicle, petrochemical and steel were the leading industries, and the pillar industry clusters included electricity, electrical appliances, machinery, chemicals, and vehicles	Export-oriented development strategy, focusing on the development of labor-intensive light industries such as textiles and footwear
1970s	The evolution of high-tech, information technology: communications equipment, computers, aerospace, bioengineering; high-tech transformation of traditional equipment and production lines and traditional products	Chemical fibers, home appliances, transportation machinery, work machinery, precision machinery, aerospace, computers, nuclear industry, synthetic materials	Transforming and deepening heavy and chemical industries, developing vehicles, steel, machinery, electronics, and shipbuilding industries
1980s		High-tech assembly processing industries represented by home appliances, vehicles and machinery	Upgrading the technologies of traditional heavy and chemical industries and forming the main export industries. Priority support to strategic industries such as fine chemicals, precision instruments, computers, electronic machinery, and aerospace, and defining emerging industries such as information, new materials and bioengineering as active industries of future development
1990s	High-tech service industries, new generation information technology, bioengineering	Service, wholesale and retail, finance and insurance, government services, real estate, transportation and communication industries; electrical machinery, transportation equipment, general machinery and other industries with comparative advantages	In the late 1990s, driven by the information industry, South Korea's production services began to develop, such as finance, insurance, real estate, transportation, warehousing and communications

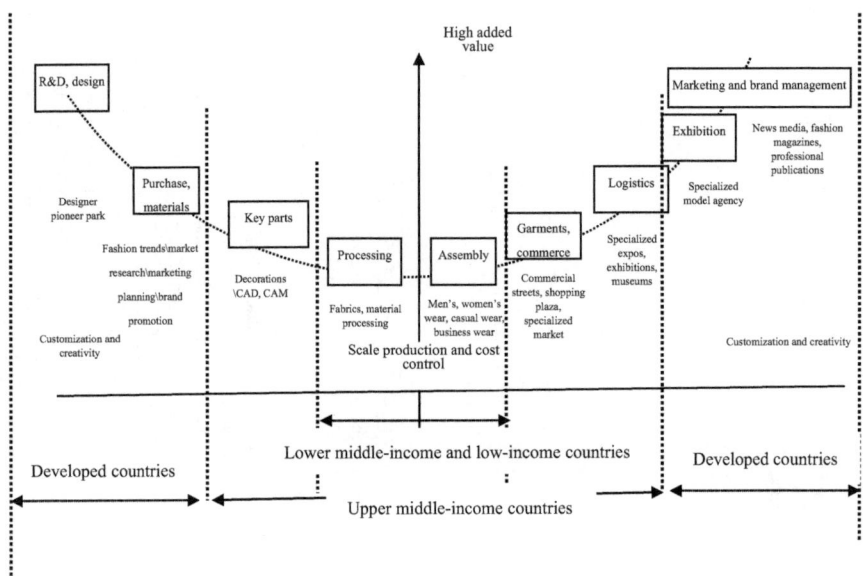

Fig. 2 International industrial division of labor and value chain (exemplified by the garment industry)

design at both ends of the smiling curve are controlled by the developed countries. Based on the past developmental foundation, the upper middle-income countries actively extend to both ends of the industry and develop into parts production, logistics, exhibitions and other fields, such as China, Mexico etc. The developed countries always control the high value-added links at both ends of the industrial chain, such as research and development, design, core key parts, brands and marketing, financial services, etc., and capture the most value of the industry. In order to leap forward to this stage of development, middle-income countries must vigorously develop their domestic brands, increase their investment in research and development and design, enhance the development of productive service industries, strive to get rid of the control of industrial chains in developed countries, seize and crowd out the profit-making space of developed countries and achieve income growth. If industrial transformation and development cannot be attained, the countries will continue to be in the low value-added link for a long time, thus resulting in economic stagnation and falling into the "middle income trap" due to the catching-up of low-income countries.

(II) **The transformation of the industrial life cycle and the impact analysis of industrial transfer on the middle-income economies**

With international industrial substitution, the developed countries always take the lead in the developmental trend of the leading international industries. In particular, after the Second World War, the accelerated development of science and technology and industry and the transformation of the life cycle of industry bring about three

Table 5 Industrial transfer introducing the life cycle theory and world system theory

Stage	Product features	Comparative advantage	Economic region	Direction of transfer
Initial	Technology-intensive	Technology	Central area	Innovation-developed
Growing	Capital-intensive	Capital	Central area	Developed-manufacturing
Mature	Labor-intensive	Labor	Semi-marginal area	Manufacturing
Declining	Labor-intensive	Labor	Marginal area	Manufacturing—underdeveloped

Note Data source Liu Yuanyuan et al., Research on Industrial Transfer of China's Processing and Manufacturing Based on the World System Theory, *Journal of Shenyang University of Technology (Social Sciences)*, 2009(18)

large-scale international industrial transfers, and different middle-income countries result in different processes of industrial transfer (Table 5).

Generally, the industries in the growth stage are subject to industrial transfer, but the declining industries are transferred often to save on costs. The initial germination and growth stage of the industries is often in the central area of the entire world economic system. In the maturing process, the developed countries in the central area start to bring about innovations to new industries, and the old industries begin to be transferred to the semi-marginal area. The industries in the declining stage are transferred from the semi-marginal area to the backward marginal area. The world economy began with the transfer of labor-intensive industries from the United States of America in the 1950s. It experienced the transfer of equipment and technology industries in the 1970s, and knowledge-intensive industries in the 1990s. Industrial transfer in different stages propelled global economic development. The first industrial transfer led to the rise of Japan. The second industrial transfer resulted in the development of the "Four Asian Tigers" such as South Korea, Taiwan, and Singapore. In the third industrial transfer, China became a global manufacturing base.

The past international industrial transfer mainly occurred in the manufacturing sector, but its connotations have been constantly changing. In terms of resource intensity, industrial transfer gradually shifted from the early labor-intensive to capital-intensive and then to technology- and knowledge-intensive industries; from the perspective of added value, they developed from low-value-added industries (such as textiles) to high value-added industries (such as integrated circuit manufacturing). It was easy to achieve a high growth rate in the early stage of development, but there was a lack of good sustainability and it was not possible to represent the direction of economic development. In the international industrial transfer, some middle-income countries did not follow the dynamic changes of international industries, and achieve their own industrial innovation and extension of the industrial chain. They were gradually abandoned by the trend of industrial transfer, and their industries fell into a low-level cycle, and the income was difficult to grow. For example, Latin American countries in the 1970s and 1980s, Southeast Asian countries in the 1980s and 1990s experienced rapid economic growth and long-term economic stagnation, and were thrown from a semi-marginal area to a marginal area. As a result, the international industrial transfer resulted from the transformation of the industrial life cycle and caused some countries to stay in the middle-income developmental stage for a long time. Therefore, clearly recognizing the change in industrial development and the division of labor in the industrial chain, closely following the leading international industries, actively expanding to the high value-added links of the industrial chain, and getting rid of the trap of the low degree of industrialization are the foundation for realizing sustainable economic development (Fig. 3).

China has long relied on the strategy of low-cost advantages and the technology of multinational corporations and lacks the independent research and development capabilities, so that industry cannot be revitalized. China is situated in the downstream of the global industrial chain and needs to adjust its economic structure. From the experience and lessons of the "middle income trap", for achieving the successful upgrading of the industrial structure, we must gain momentum to avoid the "middle income trap", that is to say, to improve the industrial structure as a breakthrough, especially the upgrading of the industrial structure, and provide new impetus for economic growth.

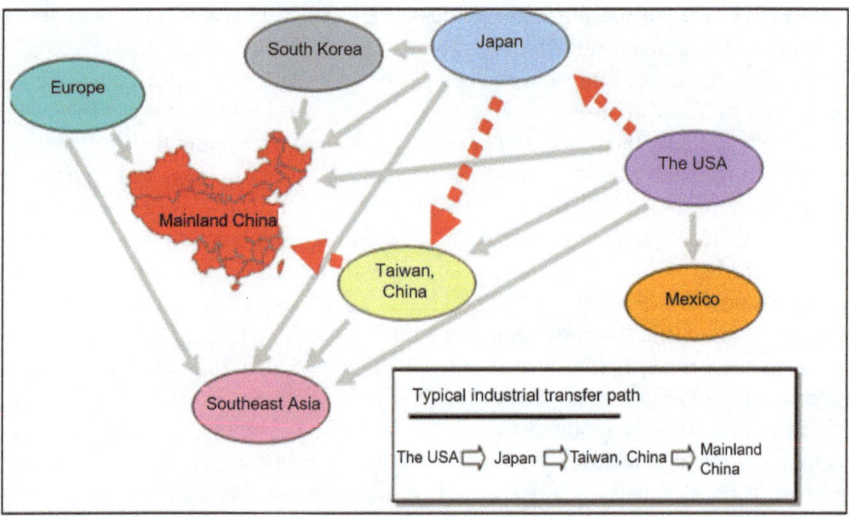

Fig. 3 The transfer of international industrial space

5 Policy Suggestions for China's Economic Transformation and Avoidance of the Middle Income Trap

At present, China is in the middle-income developmental stage, the overall quality of industrial development is not high, and it is still in the middle and low end of the global value chain. China, in the midst of leaping forward over the "middle income trap", is facing the double pressure of "suppression" by high-end industries in American and European countries and the "squeezing" effect of low-end industries in emerging countries. The traditional comparative advantages are declining, the costs of human resources are increasing, the constraints on energy resources and the ecological environment are becoming more intense, and the cost of factors is gradually rising. The developmental model that has been proved to be successful in the past and the developmental strategy promoting China's economic take-off are facing challenges from all aspects, and the industrial developmental path and industrial policy are confronted with transformational adjustment. To this end, in the critical period of transformation and development, it is necessary to accelerate the adjustment of the industrial structure and transformation and upgrading. For this purpose, attention may be paid to the following aspects:

(I) **Comprehensively adjusting the economic developmental strategy and shifting to the changes driven by innovation and guided by demand**

The export-oriented developmental strategy must be fully adjusted to change the current situation of participating in the global trade and division of labor with the comparative advantage of labor force. The dynamic comparative advantage must be developed by endogenous paths such as technology innovation and original innovation, the improvement of the overall quality of factors must be accelerated, the quality of the labor force and capital deposit should be improved, and the upgrading of industries and of the trade structure must be escalated and turned to being innovation-driven.

We must adhere to the people-oriented developmental philosophy, reverse the human-oriented means to human-oriented target, vigorously develop industries that aim for happiness and lead the transformation of industrial development through domestic demand.

(II) **Transforming the industrial developmental path and promoting industrial transformation and development**

(1) China should vigorously develop the strategic emerging industries and promote high-end industrial development. It must accelerate the adjustment of the industrial structure, seize the commanding heights of high-end industrial development, realize the high-end of key industries, and spare no efforts in developing strategic emerging industries. Not just strategic emerging industries should be developed to form new economic growth points, but also traditional industries must be transformed and upgraded to achieve industrial restructuring and upgrading, thus becoming breakthrough points and the "main engine" for transforming the economic

growth model. In terms of industry selection, we must highlight major industrial fields such as next-generation information technology, high-end equipment manufacturing, energy conservation and new energy, low-carbon and environmental protection, new materials, biopharmaceuticals, and marine economy.

(2) The productive services represented by the high-tech services must be actively developed to establish an industrial system of modern services. The high-tech services are an inevitable choice for the promotion of the continuous large-scale growth of high-tech industries and the improvement of the quality of high-tech industrial development, and to meet the urgent need to transform from "Made in China" to "Created in China". The high-tech services mainly include knowledge and talent-intensive and high-value-added industries such as information technology, biotechnology, digital content, R&D and design, intellectual property rights and the transformation of scientific and technological achievements. On the basis of increasing high-tech services, we should encourage the development of productive services such as finance and insurance, guide the life service industries to high-end consumption, build a modern service industrial system, and guide the overall structural upgrading of industries.

(III) Highlighting innovative development and promoting transformation to endogenous innovation

(1) China should strengthen the industrial innovation and technological updates in order to boost industrial upgrading. It must transform the developmental model based on simple processing and simulating innovation, adhere to independent innovation, vigorously implement the innovation-driven strategy, and promote the continuous upgrading of the industrial structure. In the key areas of information, life, new materials, new energy, etc., it should establish the national science and technology innovation system and industrialization system. The dominant role of enterprises in technology innovation and industrial transformation and upgrading must be further highlighted, and effective measures should be adopted to create a more competitive developmental environment, concentrate more innovative factors in enterprises, fully enhance the independent innovation capability of enterprises, and promote industrial transformation and upgrading. We should intensify enterprise innovation, break through core technologies in key industries, accelerate the transformation of scientific and technological achievements, and strengthen the use of information technology.

(2) China should strengthen its original innovation. Industries that pass through the middle-income stage should no longer be dominated by simple imitation and manufacturing. We need to strengthen innovation capabilities, in particular, increase research and investment in basic research and original innovation, and lay a foundation for new industries and new business forms. We should strengthen key scientific research, deepen

cooperation of industry, university and research, enhance enterprise innovation, adhere to the enterprise-dominated, market-oriented and innovative system of cooperation among industries, universities and research,
build an alliance among industries, universities and research technology
innovation, enhance the construction of carriers of the cooperation among
industries, universities and research, and accelerate the cultivation of leading innovative enterprises.

(IV) **Actively and steadily guiding the regional industrial transfer and establishing the domestic "intra-industry trade"**

China should give full play to its advantages of regional industrial differentiation, grasp the opportunities of industrial transfer from the eastern coastal areas,
and guide the industrial transfer to the central and western regions. Advantageous
and characteristic industries should be highlighted, the advantages of resources be
made full and processing trade enterprises, such as electronic information, textiles
and garments, should be developed in the central and western regions of China. The
processing trade should be guided for transformation upgrading. While carrying on
industrial transfer, we must increase policy support, encourage enterprises to use
high and new technologies to transform traditional industries, upgrade the existing
transferred industries and develop high-tech, high-value-added, fashionable and differentiated terminal products. The simple upstream and downstream division of raw
material supply and processing and manufacturing in the east and the west in the
past should be changed to achieve the intra-industry trade between among eastern,
central and western regions of China.

Cao Zhongxiong China Development Institute (Shenzhen), Ph.D., researcher, with research interests in: industrial economics.

Chapter 9
An Evolution Analysis of Regional Economic Development Disparities in Guangdong Based on the FPCA

Fan Xiaowen

Abstract The economic disparities among the Pearl River Delta and East Region, the West Region and the Mountainous Region become the primary contrasts to be urgently resolved in the economic transformation of Guangdong Province. This paper selects the added value of employees in 21 cities and applies the functional principal component analysis (FPCA) method to analyze the regional development disparities in Guangdong from 2000 to 2011. The results show that the evolution of regional disparities in Guangdong can be explained by early development disparities, disparities under the impact of the world financial crisis, and growth trend disparities formed after 2002. Compared with the period of early development, the regional disparities in Guangdong have narrowed.

Keywords FPCA · Regional disparities · Economy of Guangdong · Comparative advantage

Since the reform and opening-up, because of the difference in the relative scarcity of production factors, natural conditions and geographical locations, plus the imbalanced development policy of Guangdong Province, the regional economic development disparities and the urban-rural disparities become obvious. Guangdong is the first province to implement reform and opening-up in China and one of the most economically developed regions. However, in the transitional stage of economic development, the imbalance of regional development has deepened the contrasts of economic development. The Pearl River Delta region, covering 30.5% of the land area of the province, accounts for 79.2% of the province's total GDP. The per capita GDP is 77,637 yuan in the Pearl River Delta region, which is more than three times that of the East, West and Mountainous Regions. The regional imbalance is evident. The imbalance in regional development in Guangdong has not only deepened the contrasts of economic development, but it has also brought instability to the society. Many domestic scholars have carried out useful research and discussions on this

F. Xiaowen (✉)
China Center for Special Economic Zone Research, Shenzhen University, Shenzhen 518060, China
e-mail: fxw673@126.com

© Social Sciences Academic Press 2020
Y. Yuan (ed.), *Studies on China's Special Economic Zones 3*,
Research Series on the Chinese Dream and China's Development Path,
https://doi.org/10.1007/978-981-13-9841-4_9

topic, and proposed the method of analysis of regional disparities using the variability index [1, 2], the Theil index [3], generalized entropy, the Gini coefficient, etc. According to the results of existing research, there is still a lack of comprehensive quantitative analysis methods. This paper attempts to use the functional principal component analysis method to analyze the regional disparities and the characteristics of the evolution of economic development in Guangdong from a time and space perspective.

1 Research Ideas and Methodology

1.1 Research Ideas

The analysis of the regional disparities in Guangdong must first of all make the purpose of the study clear. Based on the results of existing research, this paper analyzes the characteristics of the evolution of regional economic development disparities. Second, the area of analysis, analytical indicators and methods of analysis of disparities are determined around this purpose.

Regions in Guangdong are usually divided into two types by administrative division and economic development. The administrative regions are divided into 21 cities, and the economic regions are divided into the Pearl River Delta Region, the East Region, the West Region and the Mountainous Region. The Pearl River Delta Region includes 9 cities, namely Guangzhou, Shenzhen, Zhuhai, Dongguan, Foshan, Zhongshan, Huizhou, Zhaoqing and Jiangmen; the East Region includes 4 cities, Shantou, Shanwei, Chaozhou and Jieyang; the West Region includes Zhanjiang, Yangjiang and Maoming; and the Mountainous Region is made up of 5 cities, Meizhou, Heyuan, Shaoguan, Yunfu and Qingyuan. Based on the feasibility of quantitative analysis data, 21 cities were selected as the research areas, and the analysis of the regional disparities was positioned to analyze the disparities among 21 cities.

At present, the indicators for examining regional disparities generally include GDP, per capita GDP, per capita disposable income, GDP growth rate, and GDP output rate per unit of land. These indicators have their own advantages and disadvantages and reflect the status of regional development according to different measures. However, from the perspective of the efficiency of economic development, per capita GDP is obviously affected by population distribution. Therefore, we use the added value created by employees as an indicator to analyze regional disparities, and the characteristics of evolution of such disparities from the differences between the added value created by employees in 21 cities.

Considering the availability and continuity of the data, combined with the government's regional development policy, 2000–2011 was selected as the research period, and the 12-year data of 21 cities formed a 12 × 21 data matrix. The data contains both time and spatial information. Functional principal component analysis (FPCA) is a method of differential analysis from a dynamic perspective. This method provides an effective perspective for exploring the structure of the data covariance matrix. It can not only extract the main differences hidden in the principal component analysis data, but also comprehensively evaluate the efficiency of the development of each city in 12 years based on the principal component score. Therefore, this paper chooses the FPCA as a method for the analysis of regional disparities.

1.2   Research Methodology—Functional Principal Component Analysis

Functional data analysis (FDA) [4, 5] is a new statistical method proposed by Canadian statisticians Ramsay and Dalzell (1991). Unlike previous studies, discrete data are regarded as the functional data (curves) of time. Although the added value of employees in the analysis index is obtained at each discrete time point, since the variation is inherently dynamic, it is theoretically possible to estimate the function value $x(t)$ at any time point t. Therefore, we can convert it into functional data, that is, the analysis index of each city is converted into a function, and there are 21 function curves for 21 cities. On this basis, these function curves are analyzed.

The Functional Principal Component Analysis (FPCA) is similar to the Principal Component Analysis (PCA) method in traditional multivariate statistics. The steps of the analysis are as follows:

Step 1: convert discrete data into functional data.

Select a group of B-spline bases, $\phi_j(t)$, $j = 1, 2, \ldots, n$ $i = 1, 2, \ldots, m$

$$x_i(t) = \sum_{j=1}^{n_b} \beta_j \phi_j(t) \tag{1}$$

In Eq. (1), $x_i(t)$ represents the variable function (smooth curve) that varies with time, n_b is the number of basis functions, m represents the number of regions, and β_j is the coefficient in the basis expansion. Usually, the least squares method is used to determine β_j, i.e.

$$\min \sum_{j=1}^{n} [y_{ij} - x_i(t)]^2 \quad j = 1, 2, \ldots, n; \quad i = 1, 2, \ldots, m \tag{2}$$

In Eq. (2), y_{ij} indicates the variable observed value of each region in a certain period of time, and n is the number of observed values in each region. $x_i(t)$ can be obtained after estimating β_j.

In order to estimate β_j and obtain the function curves for variable analysis, this study selects the second-order differential roughness penalty and applies the least squares criterion to estimate β_j, namely

$$\min \theta_\lambda(\beta) = \sum_{j=1}^{n} [y_i - x_i(t)]^2 + \lambda \int [D^2 x_i(t)]^2 dt \qquad (3)$$

In Eq. (3), λ is the smooth parameter that needs to be given in advance. We take $\lambda = 10^{-4}$, and then obtain the function $x_i(t)$ after estimating β_j.

In Step 2, the FPCA is performed on the estimated functional data.

The model uses the smooth function PCA, and the mathematical model of the first principal component obtained using the roughness penalty method is:

$$f_{i1} = \int \eta_1(t) x_i(t) dt \qquad (4)$$

$\eta(t)$ is the principal component weight function, which corresponds to the weight vector of the principal component in traditional multivariate statistics. Each principal component is determined by a principal component weight function $\eta_1(t)$, and $\eta(t)$ is a function of time t. Satisfy:

$$\int \{\eta_1(t)\}^2 dt + \lambda \int \{\eta_1''(t)\}^2 dt = 1$$
$$\max \sum f_{i1}^2 / n \qquad (5)$$

Similarly, calculate the kth principal component weight function $\eta_k(t)$ to get the principal component score f_{ik}:

$$f_{ik} = \int \eta_k(t) x_i(t) dt \qquad (6)$$

Satisfy:

$$\int \{\eta_k(t)\}^2 dt + \lambda \int \{\eta_k''(t)\}^2 dt = 1$$
$$\int \eta_k(t)\eta_1(t) dt + \lambda \int \eta_k''(t)\eta_1''(t) dt = \cdots = \int \eta_k(t)\eta_{k-1}(t) dt$$
$$+ \lambda \int \eta_k''(t)\eta_{k-1}''(t) dt = 0$$
$$\max \sum f_{ik}^2 / n \qquad (7)$$

2   Empirical Analysis

Comparing the regional GDP of 21 cities in Guangdong from 2000 to 2011 to the corresponding number of employees, the 12×21 data matrix of added value per employee can be obtained. According to the above analysis model, according to the functional data analysis program based on R software, the data matrix is analyzed by FPCA in R software. The results are as follows:

Figure 1 shows the B-spline basis for converting data into functional data. Figure 2 shows the function curve of added value of employees in the 21 cities from 2000 to 2011 after conversion to functional data. Based on the functional data, the principal component analysis is carried out. The results of the calculation indicate that two principal components are extracted, and the variance contribution rates are 50.9% and 48.2%, respectively, and the cumulative contribution rate is 99.1%. The corresponding feature values are 7.204205e-01 and 2.474675e-02, respectively.

The solid line in Fig. 3 represents the first principal component weight function, and the broken line represents the second principal component weight function. The larger the value of the principal component weight, the greater the disparities between the cities during this period. The evolution of the disparities between the 21 cities can be analyzed and determined by two curves. Combined with Figs. 4 and 5, we can more intuitively observe the evolution of the disparities in the regional development in Guangdong.

The functional principal components are calculated after the centralized processing of data. In order to better understand the meaning of the principal components, based on the mean of the function curves of 21 cities, the appropriate multiples of the principal component weighting function are added or subtracted respectively to plot Figs. 4 and 5, which comprise three curves each. In Figs. 4 and 5, the solid lines

Fig. 1 B-spline basis function

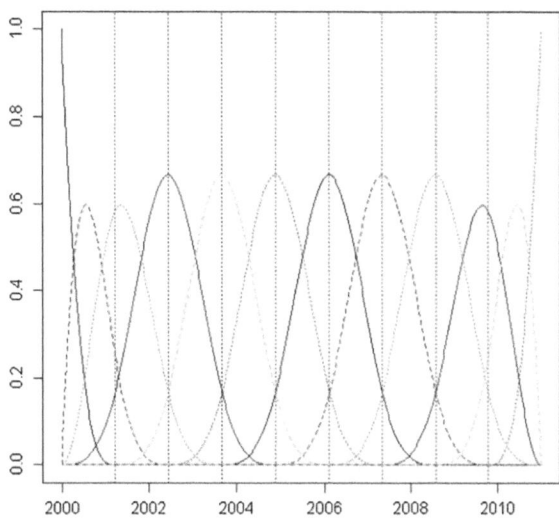

Fig. 2 Smooth function
curve of added value of
employees

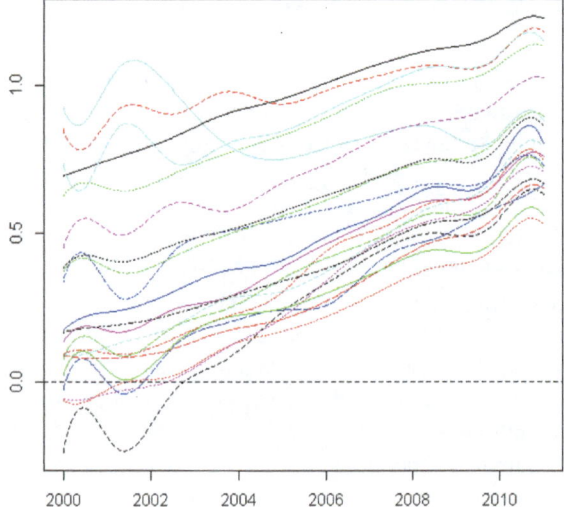

Fig. 3 Principal component
weight function graph

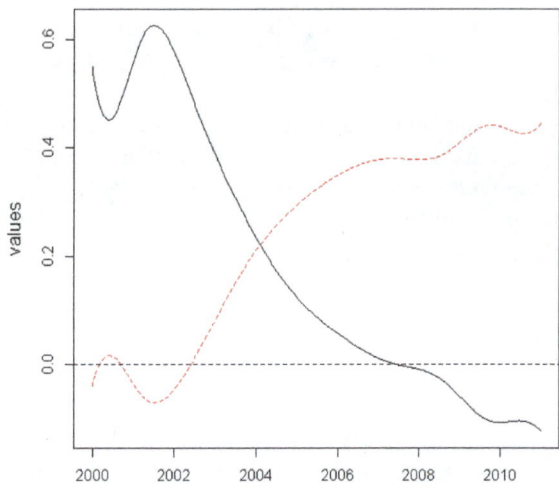

represent the mean curves, the "+" curves represent the curves formed by adding
appropriate times of the mean line, and the "−" curves represent the curve after
subtracting the appropriate times. The farther the "+" curves or "−" curves are from
the mean line, the greater the difference. The "+" curves above the mean curve indicate that the indicators of the analysis are positively affected during a certain period
of time, and below the mean curve indicate that the indicators of the analysis are
affected by negative factors during a certain period of time. The scores reflect the
development of the primary components, with a mean value of zero.

The first principal component reflects the differences in the efficiency of the economic development of 21 cities in Guangdong due to early development disparities

Fig. 4 First principal
component

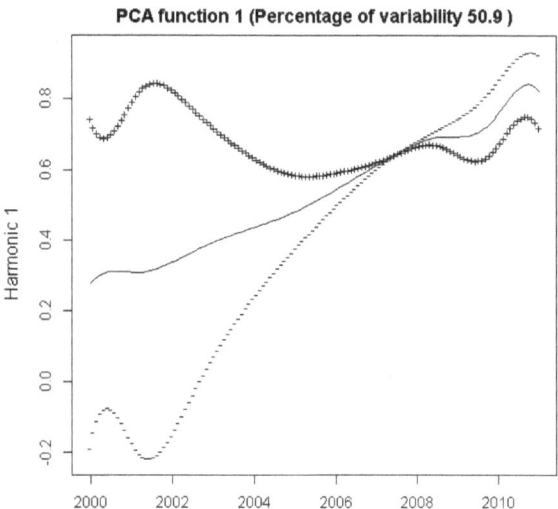

Fig. 5 Second principal
component

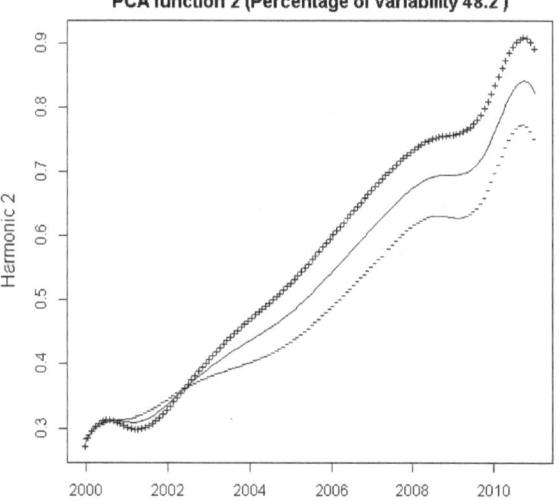

and later impacts from the financial crisis. It can be seen from Fig. 4 that before 2002, the differences between the added values of employees in various cities of Guangdong were large, and then began to decrease. However, the financial crisis that started in late 2007 had a negative impact on the added value of employees, and the differences of the cities once again increased. Among them, Dongguan, which had the highest score of the first primary component, and Heyuan, which had the lowest score, were the most representative. In 2002, the added value of employees in Dongguan reached 114,000 yuan/person, and in 2011 it was 75,300 yuan/person, which indicates that the early development of Dongguan was good with bigger "innovation profits". With the rapid development of other regions and the impact of the international financial crisis, the sustainability was bad. The per capita added value of Heyuan in 2002 was 7180 yuan/person, which was the lowest in Guangdong, and it was 42,800 yuan/person in 2011. Although there was growth after 2002 and it was less affected by the financial crisis after 2008, its economic development still lagged far behind other regions and belonged to the underdeveloped regions with low added value.

The second principal component reflects the evolution of disparities in the growth trends of the 21 cities in Guangdong after 2002. As can be seen from Fig. 3, the disparities in added value of employees in these cities rapidly expanded from 2002 to 2006, and the expansion has become relatively stable since 2007. The most representative cities were Guangzhou with the highest score of the primary component and Meizhou with the lowest score. In Guangzhou, the added value of employees was low before 2002. In 2002, it was 62,300 yuan/person, and then increased rapidly. In 2011, it was 167,200 yuan/person. The second principal component score was 1.18, indicating that Guangzhou's innovation was continuously improving and economic efficiency continued to increase. In Meizhou, the added value of employees was 10,200 yuan/person in 2002 and 33,800 yuan/person in 2011. The second principal component score was -0.823, indicating that Meizhou was a slowly developed and inefficient underdeveloped region.

The results of the FPCA show that since 2000, the regional disparities reflected by the added value of employees in 21 cities in Guangdong can be analyzed from two perspectives: disparities formed during the early development and those due to the impact of the financial crisis, and those formed in the growth trends since late 2002.

Figure 6 shows the scatter plot of the Component 1 Score and the Component 2 Score for 21 cities, which are mainly distributed in the first quadrant and the third quadrant. The Component 1 Score and Component 2 Score of the cities in the first quadrant are higher than the average level, and belong to developed regions with high added value. The Component 1 Score and Component 2 Score of the cities in the third quadrant are lower than the average level, and belong to the underdeveloped regions with low added value.

Nine cities are located in the first quadrant: Guangzhou, Shenzhen, Foshan, Zhuhai, Zhongshan, Dongguan, Huizhou, Jiangmen and Shantou, including 8 Pearl River Delta cities except Zhaoqing. Shantou, as a special economic zone, has a Component 1 Score of 0.12 and a Component 2 Score of -0.004, which are close to 0, so the city falls in the first quadrant. Among them, Guangzhou, Shenzhen, Foshan and Zhuhai have a relatively high degree of economic efficiency and small differences. These cities had a larger per capita added value in the early period, which further increased later. As the leading cities in the Pearl River Delta and even Guangdong, they are known as developed regions. Zhongshan, Huizhou, Jiangmen and Shantou are slightly inferior to those leading cities, so they are known as sub-developed regions. Dongguan in the first quadrant is special, the highest Component 1 Score indicates that it developed well in the early period, but the lower Component 2 Score

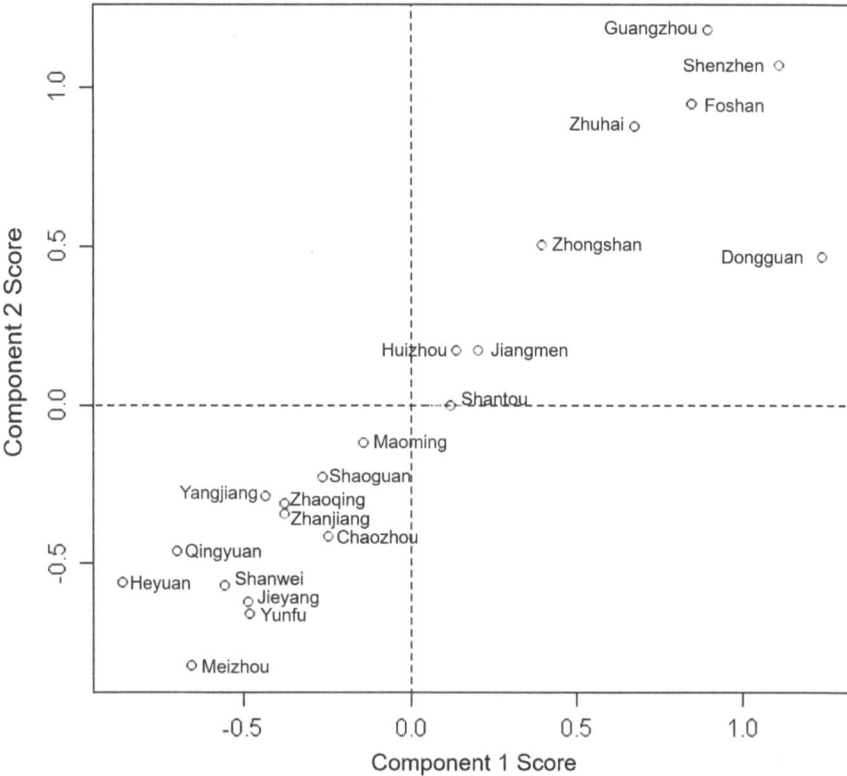

Fig. 6 Principal component scores

shows that its development has not been further improved in the later period, thus lagging behind the leading cities. It is classified into the sub-developed regions.

For 12 cities in the third quadrant, Maoming, Shaoguan, Yangjiang, Zhanjiang, Zhaoqing and Chaozhou are relatively close to each other and are known as underdeveloped regions; and Heyuan, Qingyuan, Shanwei, Jieyang, Yunfu and Meizhou are close to each other and are known as the least underdeveloped regions. Shantou, Maoming and Shaoguan are the leading cities of the East, West and Mountainous Regions.

The Component 1 Score F1 and the Component 2 Score F2 are respectively weighted by the variance contribution rate, and the comprehensive score Z of the efficiency of development of 21 cities can be obtained as shown in Table 1.

$$z = 0.514F_1 + 0.486F_2$$

According to the comprehensive score, although Shenzhen ranks first, it is mainly due to its rapid development in the early stage. Guangzhou shows a tendency to climb to the top. From the perspective of per capita added value, Shenzhen's future tasks

Table 1 Principal component scores and comprehensive scores of 21 cities

City	Component 1 score	Component 2 score	Comprehensive score
Shenzhou	1.106	1.068	1.088
Guangzhou	0.891	1.181	1.032
Foshan	0.845	0.950	0.896
Dongguan	1.238	0.468	0.863
Zhuhai	0.674	0.880	0.774
Zhongshan	0.396	0.501	0.447
Jiangmen	0.202	0.171	0.187
Huizhou	0.135	0.171	0.153
Shantou	0.120	−0.004	0.060
Maoming	−0.144	−0.117	−0.131
Shaoguan	−0.263	−0.226	−0.245
Chaozhou	−0.249	−0.414	−0.329
Zhaoqing	−0.378	−0.309	−0.345
Zhanjiang	−0.378	−0.343	−0.361
Yangjiang	−0.435	−0.289	−0.364
Jieyang	−0.486	−0.619	−0.551
Shanwei	−0.556	−0.568	−0.562
Yunfu	−0.485	−0.658	−0.569
Qingyuan	−0.703	−0.459	−0.584
Heyuan	−0.869	−0.560	−0.719
Meizhou	−0.659	−0.823	−0.739

are still very difficult. How to further improve the technological content and make products with high added value are the urgent tasks faced by the 21 cities. It can be easily observed from the evaluation scores that the disparities are objective and there is still a long way to go to reach balanced regional development.

3   Conclusions

To conclude, from the perspective of the future regional development in Guangdong, the disparities of 21 cities objectively exist. It is the regional developmental disparities between the Pearl River Delta and the East, West and Mountainous Regions and the disparities within the regions that form the respective comparative advantages of the 21 cities. The existence of a comparative advantage provides opportunities and possibilities for backward areas to catch up with developed regions, and theoretically provides the possibility of narrowing regional disparities. We should correctly analyze and understand regional developmental disparities in Guangdong and take the initiative to respond to the transformation of economic development. The backward areas should make good use of their "late-mover advantage" and acquire the knowledge and experience of the developed areas at a lower cost. With Shantou, Maoming and Shaoguan as leading cities for the development of the East, West and Mountainous Regions, disparities with the developed regions are narrowed and this is the path and strategy for achieving coordinated regional development in Guangdong.

References

1. Wen Ruihong, Relations of Economic Growth and Regional Economic Disparities in Guangdong [J], *Geography and Geo-information Science*, 2012(1).
2. *Statistical Yearbook of Guangdong Province 2012*, http://www.gdstats.gov.cn/.
3. Luo Hao, A Positive Study on the Variation of Regional Disparities in Guangdong Province *China Population, Resources and Environment*, 2003(6).
4. J.O. Ramsay, B.W. Silverman, Functional Data Analysis[M](Second Edition), Foreign Famous Works Series (Photocopies) 12, Science Press, 2006.
5. J.O. Ramsay, B.W. Silverman, Applied Functional Data Analysis: Methods and Case Studies [M], Springer, 2002.

Fan Xiaowen Associate Professor of the China Center for Special Economic Zone Research, Shenzhen University, Ph.D., in Economics, with research interests in SEZ economics and econometrics.

Chapter 10
Research on the Regional Industrial Coordinated Development and Spatial Distribution Strategy

Liu Jing

Abstract Based on the theory of endogenous growth, the formation and evolution of the inter-regional division of labor and trade relations and the exploration of the new theory of economic geography, we empirically analyzed and investigated the intrinsic law of coordinated development of regional industries and reasonable spatial layout. The data of the Pearl River Delta from 2002 to 2010 and Shenzhen, Dongguan and Huizhou from 2004 to 2010 were selected to analyze the panel data model. The empirical analysis indicated that the industrial similarity of the Pearl River Delta had a positive relationship with economic growth. The system of estimation of the degree of coordination of regional industrial development was constructed, and the results revealed that the overall coordination of manufacturing development in Shenzhen, Dongguan and Huizhou showed a good upward trend. Taking Shenzhen, Dongguan and Huizhou as an example, we explored the coordinated development of regional industries and spatial layout strategies, and proposed a reasonable layout of large-scale industrial clusters and related policy suggestions based on the developmental strategy of city clusters, with a view to providing new ideas for the sustainable growth of regional economy with endogenous dynamics.

Keywords Regional industries · Coordination · Spatial layout · Industrial cluster · Strategy

1 Research Question

Coordinated industrial development and spatial layout are located at the core of regional development. At present, the domestic and international economic landscape has undergone profound changes. Many enterprises are faced with the risks of changes in the RMB exchange rate, intensifying market competitions, high labor costs and other internal and external dilemmas, which have formed a mechanism

L. Jing (✉)
Institute of Hong Kong, Macao & SEZs Economy, Jinan University,
Guangzhou 510632, China
e-mail: liujingwuerjiao@126.com

© Social Sciences Academic Press 2020
Y. Yuan (ed.), *Studies on China's Special Economic Zones 3*,
Research Series on the Chinese Dream and China's Development Path,
https://doi.org/10.1007/978-981-13-9841-4_10

for reversed transmission of pressure. In this macroscopic environment, it is of great significance to discuss the regional industrial coordination and spatial layout. Due to the very close proximity in geography and space, the Pearl River Delta has strong similarities in the stage of economic development. Moreover, since the enterprises in the Pearl River Delta mostly have a similar cultural background, there has long been controversy about the assimilation of industrial structure in this region. The mainstream view holds that the industrial structure of the Pearl River Delta has a high degree of convergence, and in most cases, this convergence means the repeated construction of different regions, which is a serious waste of resources. According to the estimation of the *2009 Guangdong Provincial Situation Survey Report*, among the three economic circles of Shenzhen-Dongguan-Huizhou (SDH), Zhuhai-Zhongshan-Jiangmen (ZZJ) and Guangzhou-Foshan-Zhaoqing (GFZ), the index of industrial similarity of SDH is the highest with an average value of 0.88. The average similarity index value is 0.72 for ZZJ and 0.49 for GFZ. From 1998 to 2007, the industrial similarity of the SDH economic circle only drops from 0.9 to 0.88, that of ZZJ falls from 0.84 to 0.71 and that of GFZ decreases from 0.63 to 0.49. Accordingly, this report concludes that: Industrial similarity is a serious problem faced by the three major economic circles, in particular, the SDH economic circle. However, recently the point of view that there is no serious industrial similarity in the Pearl River Delta has become more prevailing. On the contrary, the industrial structure of the Pearl River Delta is improving in terms of division of labor and coordination, and the evolution of industrial division of labor in this region is closely related to the behaviors of local governments [1, 2]. In view of the above analysis, this paper starts with the similarity of the industrial structural of the Pearl River Delta, attempts to find the theoretical basis from the theoretical review, and integrates the empirical study to explore the coordinated development of regional industries and the strategy of spatial layout.

2 Theoretical Origin of Industrial Coordinated Development and Spatial Layout

Tracing the evolution of the regional division of labor and trade theory and its development, based on the endogenous growth theory, this paper explores the evolution of the theory of division of labor and trade and its relations with the industrial spatial layout-related theories and up until the new theory of economic geography, and it seeks the point of convergence from theories relevant to the division of labor, trade and spatial layout of endogenous growth, and thus finding the ways to solve the practical problems.

2.1   The Evolution and Development of Regional Division of Labor and Trade Theories

International trade theory has long been the most influential theory used by regional economists to explain inter-regional division of labor and trading activities. From Adam Smith's classical theory of trade up to the new theory of trade represented by Paul R. Krugman, they can be regarded as the main origins of the inter-regional division of labor and trade theory. It is worth mentioning that Krugman introduced the concept of space into the normative framework of economic research. Based on the market structure of monopolistic competition and the increasing returns hypothesis, Krugman effectively integrated the location theory, the inter-regional division of labor theory, the trade theory with the regional developmental theory, and formed a new school of economic geography. He interpreted regional development as a self-reinforcing process of economic space driven by external economies of scale (market externalities), a certain contingent and uncertainty factors, historical and special events, certain preferences, and the natural availability of certain production factors may tend to be magnified in the process of self-reinforcement and have a decisive effect on the formation of the regional landscape and the development of the regional economy; once the economic landscape has been formed, it will generate the cumulative effects through the forward and backward linkages of production and flow of factors, so that the irrational economic distribution has a "locking in" effect. In the real world, the trend of automatically moving to the optimal spatial landscape does not exist [3]. Regional economic development has a strong dependence on the path. With the development of the world's economic liberalization and globalization, domestic trade and international trade are increasingly integrated: some new trade theories begin to pay attention to the impact of domestic trade on international trade, not only from the national perspective, but more importantly, investigating the reasons for international trade from the perspectives of industries and enterprises. Professor Michael E. Porter from Harvard Business School held the opinion that a country's competitive advantage is gained through creation, and the key to its formation lies in the establishment and innovation of advantageous industries [4]. Compared with the strategic trade policy, Porter's "National Competitive Advantage Theory" puts forward some ideas that are more realistic for the developing countries. According to Porter, the competitiveness of a country does not necessarily lie in the entire national economy, but mainly depends on whether there are some unique industries or industrial clusters in the country. That is to say, the country's competitive advantage is usually in some unique industrial sectors, the so-called industries with competitive advantage. The same is true for a region. Porter's national competitive advantage depends primarily on factors in the "national diamond" system. In his opinion, there are four pillars affecting the competitive advantage of development and the industries of a country or a region, namely "factor conditions, demand conditions, related and supporting industries, firm structure, strategy and rivalry", which promote and restrict each other and form the "diamond model". An important development of

Porter's competitive advantage theory is combining the theory of competitive advantage with the location theory (economic geography), proposing the concept of cluster, and calling it "New Economics of Competition" [5]. Cluster is a common feature of industries with an international competitive advantage, which are usually concentrated in specific geographic regions. The competitive advantage of clusters of Porter is based on the competitive advantage of the direct economic factors. Through geographical concentration and optimization of industrial organizations, the industrial clusters obtain the competitive advantage of economic factors.

2.2 Division of Labor and Trade Under the Theory of Endogenous Growth

Generally speaking, factors affecting the inter-regional division of labor and trade can be divided into exogenous factors that are not dependent on the division of labor and endogenous factors that are formed in the evolution of the division of labor. Yang [6] also divided the comparative advantage into endogenous comparative advantages and exogenous comparative advantage by their generation before or during the division of labor. In this sense, economies of scale and competitive advantage can be seen as an important aspect of the formation of comparative advantage. It can be found that the economies of scale are also an important reason for trade. Due to the existence of economies of scale, two regions with the same production and resource conditions can also benefit from the trade. This trade advantage based on economies of scale without the need for exogenous comparative advantage is also known as acquired comparative advantage. Since the innate comparative advantage cannot be evolved, it seldom has meaning in terms of economic growth; and the comparative advantage depends on correct decision-making, which can promote the further improvement of productivity. Therefore, this acquired comparative advantage can be used to explain economic growth [7].

Exogenous factors refer to the natural and historical conditions objectively existing in the region, and are exogenous variables of regional economic development. Exogenous factors are the basic premise of inter-regional division of labor and trade. In particular, the early inter-regional division of labor is mainly based on differences in natural conditions. Even in modern economic activities, these exogenous variables such as natural resources, regional conditions, population and labor resources, and culture as the carrier of historical knowledge are still important factors in determining the inter-regional division of labor. Exogenous factors are an important source of the regional exogenous comparative advantage. The so-called exogenous comparative advantage refers to the benefits of trade generated in a certain region due to prior productivity differences or resource differences. In the early stage of economic development, the inter-regional division of labor is based mainly on exogenous comparative advantages, especially exogenous resource advantages. In the traditional agricultural society, due to the low level of productivity, high transaction costs, and underdeveloped division of labor and commodity exchanges, the scale of economic agglomeration, the influence of cities and the local economic linkages are limited, and a large number of self-sufficient local economies exist in isolation [8]. In this stage, the division of labor and trade among regions is mainly based on surplus primary products. Endogenous factors refer to variables that the regional economic system itself can determine during a period. These factors are determined by the interaction of specialized decisions of the profit-making individual economic entities in the process of the endogenous evolution of the internal and external division of labor. Because people have different levels of understanding of economic development, the endogenous variables that people recognize are different. For example, technology, systems, etc. were not considered economically endogenous in the past. Endogenous factors determine the endogenous comparative advantage of the region. The so-called endogenous comparative advantage refers to the difference in post-regional productivity caused by the decision to choose different directions in the evolution of the division of labor. The new classical economics holds that as the efficiency of transaction continues to improve, the evolution of the division of labor will be accompanied by changes in economic development, trade, and market structure. Specifically, each person's level of specialization, productivity, trade dependence, degree of commodification, concentration of production, degree of marketization, degree of diversification of economic structure, and degree of interdependence among people are all important endogenous factors in the evolution of the division of labor [7]. Further, technology and institutions are also important factors in determining the endogenous comparative advantage of inter-regional division of labor. Endogenous comparative advantage will be continuously created and promoted with the development of the division of labor, and also largely determines the division of labor in the next stage.

The experimentation in social organization is a key part in the evolution of the division of labor and specialization. Because in the initial self-sufficient economy, although practice can improve the ability to pay for labor productivity and transaction costs, laborers do not know whether they can increase the net income after the division of labor. Then, someone needs to do an experiment. Therefore, Yang Xiaokai and Huang Youguang proposed a model for experiments in social organization. Before the division of labor begins, all the same people are totally self-sufficient, and they do not know relative prices and the real income of various commodities under different divisions of labor. Suppose that people need a period of time and a certain fee to find the relative price under a division of labor structure through bargaining or the Walras negative feedback mechanism, and once people know the price and have calculated the real income under each possible professional choice, they can immediately choose the profession with the highest real income. Each stage of the experiment in social organization can generate some new organizational information about the effective division of labor, and each decision-maker can re-adjust his/her next dynamic decision about the organizational experiment based on such information. This means that if the new mode is not as effective as the previously known division of labor, people can immediately return to the original mode. If its utility exceeds the original division of labor mode, then people will choose the new division of labor mode.

In short, in the early stage of the development of the division of labor, exogenous factors are the driving force of the inter-regional division of labor, but with the development of the economy and the improvement in the efficiency of the transaction, the role of exogenous factors in inter-regional division of labor is getting smaller and smaller, but endogenous factors such as knowledge and technology play an increasingly important role in the formation and development of the regional competitive advantage. The development of regional economy is increasingly dependent on, and also fundamentally derived from, the role of endogenous factors. That is to say, in an economic system where the division of labor is becoming detailed and organized, the region can obtain endogenous comparative advantage and sustainable economic and social development mainly through specialization.

2.3 Origins of the Theory of Industrial Spatial Layout: From Trade Theory to the New Theory of Economic Geography

As early as half a century ago, Isard (1956) claimed that the trade theory and the location theory were two sides of the same coin [9]. Ohlin [10] also emphasized that the industrial location theory and the trade theory should be combined to better explain the industrial location and inter-regional trade patterns. Krugman mentioned in the beginning part of the division of geography and trade that about a year ago, he suddenly realized that as an international economist, during most of his career, he thought and wrote about economic geography, but he did not realize that for the theoretical interpretation of industrial geography, the neo-classical trade theory emphasized the regional differences of the factor endowments, the new trade theory introduced the market effects of economies of scale and imperfect competition, while the new economic geography emphasized the increasing returns to scale, demand linkage effects, cost linkage effects and accumulative circulation mechanism etc. [11]. On a perfectly competitive market, for homogenous products and under the framework of traditional economics of constant returns to scale, the neoclassical trade theory holds the view that decisions and choices regarding enterprise location depend on the comparative advantage, which stems from the spatial distribution of capital, technology, resource endowments, etc. The dominant location mode is the specialized divisions of labor among industries. If there is no difference in technology and resource endowments, the industries will be evenly distributed in space. In addition, since the neoclassical trade model assumes that there is no cost of trade, the demand does not affect the industrial location, but the neoclassical trade theory cannot explain the regional industrial division of labor with similar resource endowments and technical levels, nor can it explain the division of labor and trade within the industry, or the division of labor within the region.

Under the hypotheses of a monopolistic competitive market and differentiated products, the new trade theory emphasizes that economies of scale can promote international trade even when there are no resource and technological differences

[12], and at the same time can trigger changes in manufacturing geography. In order to achieve economies of scale, enterprises are concentrated in a few locations; in order to reduce transportation costs, enterprises are concentrated in the location with the best market accessibility, and the realization of economies of scale is closely related to the market demand of products. The market scale effect also determines and affects the industrial location. If the enterprises are facing serious trade barriers, industrial activities are scattered; as the trade costs decrease, production activities with economies of scale are close to the consumer market [12]. Anyway, in the context of an integrated market, industries with increasing economies of scale become more concentrated. It is further assumed that there is no spatial difference between resource endowments and technology, but the labor force can be migrant. The new model of economic geography completely internalizes the industrial location, and the industrial geography depends on the interaction between transportation costs and economies of scale [13]. In addition to the role of economies of scale, the inter-industry demand linkages motivate end-products and intermediate producers to approach product purchasers (i.e., backward linkages) while the transportation cost linkages cause the consumers of final products and intermediate products to be spatially close to their suppliers (i.e., forward linkages), thus leading to a self-accumulating process, promoting industrial spatial distribution along a certain path, and finally achieving a state of regional equilibrium. This state depends on the initial spatial distribution and industrial characteristics [14]. There is an inverted U-shaped relationship between industrial spatial concentration and trade costs, and the intermediate level of trade costs leads to the most concentrated industrial distribution. Moreover, the new geography of economics has also found some factors that may lead to industrial dispersion, such as factor cost differences, final demand and the immovability of the land factor, diseconomies of agglomeration and low wages.

As stated above, the neo-classical theory of trade emphasizes the influence of first nature advantages on industrial spatial layout, and considers that the factor supply determines the industrial location; the new trade and new model of economic geography finds that the second nature advantages can promote the geographical concentration of industries and the product demand becomes an important location factor. The new theory of trade and the new economic geography are based on the same framework of research, but one emphasizes the international commodity flow and the other focuses on the domestic labor flow. The conclusions of the models are all ascribed to the industrial spatial layout. Obviously, in reality, the industrial spatial layout should be the result of the combination of first nature advantages and second nature advantages. The foreign trade industry linkages and factor flows constitute the second nature advantages, which is the focus of this paper.

3 Process of Empirical Research and Interpretation of the Results

3.1 Some Empirical Research on Industrial Similarity and Economic Growth

1. Research samples

A further empirical analysis is prepared by integrating the analysis of the mechanism of similarity of industrial structure described by the above models. In terms of industry selection, considering that agriculture and service industries rely heavily on natural resources, the natural environment and population distribution, and the secondary industry is relatively less dependent on natural resources, this paper makes an analysis of the differences in the regional industrial structure based on the secondary industry. For the selection of the time period, considering that the reform of China's administrative decentralization was carried out from 1980 to 1994, the real change in the central and local power structure actually started after the 1994 tax reform, and the process of economic integration in the Pearl River Delta was rapidly advanced only in the early 21st century, for the consistency of statistics, this paper selects the data for 9 years from 2002 to 2010 as the period of research. Thus, the samples of this research are the 9-year data variable in 9 cities of the Pearl River Delta.

2. Variable data

For the Dissimilarity of Industrial Structure, this paper refers to Krugman's [15] method of index measurement for this variable:

$$Ynm, t = \left| \frac{Yin, t}{Yn, t} - \frac{Yim, t}{Ym, t} \right| \tag{3}$$

In Eq. (3), $n, m = 1, 2, 3, n \neq m$. n, m represents the region, which specifically refers to the nine cities in the Pearl River Delta: Guangzhou, Shenzhen, Zhuhai, Jiangmen, Huizhou, Zhongshan, Foshan, Zhaoqing and Dongguan, t represents time, i represents industry, and $Y_{nm,t}$ represents the overall situation of industrial similarity of the regions n, m in the t period. Further, the coefficient of the similarity of industrial structure is also an important method of measurement, which is used in this analysis too. The specific equation is:

$$Sij = \sum_{k=1}^{n} (xik \cdot xjk) / \sqrt{\sum_{k=1}^{n} x_{ik}^2 \sum_{k=1}^{n} x_{jk}^2} \tag{4}$$

In Eq. (4), i and j are regions, n is industry, and $S_{ij} \in (0, 1)$. This equation indicates that the greater the coefficient of the similarity of the industrial structure, the stronger the industrial similarity [6]. When using Eqs. (3) and (4) for calculation, all data are taken from the *Yangtze River Delta and Pearl River Delta and Hong Kong & Macao SAR & Taiwan Statistical Yearbook* as well as the *Guangdong Statistical Yearbook*, and some missing data come from the statistical yearbooks of these cities in the corresponding years.

3. Statistical description

First, with Eq. (3), we use the relevant data of 9 cities in the Pearl River Delta from 2002 to 2010 to calculate the difference of industrial structure. The detailed results are shown in Annex 1. The results indicate that the industrial structure of Guangzhou and Zhaoqing is quite different from other cities. This means that the phenomenon of industrial similarity in the Pearl River Delta seems to be intensified. Although resource endowments of the Pearl River Delta are largely homogeneous, and most cities regard the electronics, automobile, machinery, chemical and pharmaceutical industries as the leading industries for future development, from the perspective of industrial division of labor, the differences of industrial structure are being reduced among some regions, while they are being enlarged among other regions. This fully demonstrates that the industrial division of labor has played a role in the adjustment of industrial structure in various regions. Therefore, the intensification of regional competition is normal, a normal phenomenon of the market economy.

According to Eq. (4) and using the relevant data of 9 cities from 2002 to 2010, we calculate the coefficient of the similarity of industrial structure of the Pearl River Delta. The detailed data is shown in Annex 2. We find that the coefficients of similarity of the second industry structure of 9 cities are very close, and have an increasing trend with the passage of time. In recent years, criticisms about industrial similarity and redundant construction in the Pearl River Delta have been heard incessantly. A lot of studies point out that the advantageous industries of the nine cities in the Pearl River Delta are basically the same, and the coefficient of similarity of the secondary industry is relatively high.

Is this higher industrial similarity not conducive to the inter-regional complementarity and division of labor and cooperation and the realization of the Pearl River Delta integration? Will the industrial similarity also have its reasonableness and inevitability? The industrial convergence can form an industrial cluster to some extent, so that the industries in the Pearl River Delta agglomerate. With the above questions in mind, we make a regression of GDP growth rate and coefficient of similarity of industrial structure of the Pearl River Delta.

As shown in Table 1, through processing the coefficient of the similarity of the structure and the data for the GDP growth rate of the Pearl River Delta, we find that there is a nonlinear relationship between the GDP growth rate and the coefficient of the similarity of the industrial structure, so the coefficient of the similarity of the industrial structure (SC) and its quadratic term (SC2) are included in the explanatory variables. We have the following equation:

4. Analysis of the results

Through calculations, as shown in Table 2, it has been found that GDP growth rates are positive. That is to say, the coefficient of the similarity of the industrial

Table 1 Coefficient of structure similarity and GDP growth rate of the Pearl River Delta

Year	Coefficient of the similarity of industrial structure	GDP growth rate
2002	0.917056	0.138
2003	0.952389	0.166
2004	0.945278	0.16
2005	0.925083	0.158
2006	0.930028	0.169
2007	0.93275	0.162
2008	0.939472	0.161
2009	0.928028	0.153
2010	0.956083	0.164

Data Source The coefficient of the similarity of industrial structure is obtained by calculation; the GDP growth rate comes from the *Yangtze River Delta and Pearl River Delta and Hong Kong & Macao SAR & Taiwan Statistical Yearbook*, and some missing data are extracted from the *Guangdong Statistical Yearbook* of the corresponding years

Table 2 Impact of the coefficient of the similarity of the industrial structure of the Pearl River Delta on the GDP growth rate

Variable	Coefficient	Std. error	t-Statistic	Prob.
C	−28.3744	12.40858	−2.28668	0.0622
SC	60.42515	26.47385	2.282447	0.0626
SC2	−31.9826	14.11863	−2.26528	0.0641
R-squared	0.689049	Mean dependent var	0.159	
Adjusted R-squared	0.585399	S.D. dependent var	0.009124	
S.E. of regression	0.005875	Akaike info criterion	−7.17502	
Sum squared resid	0.000207	Schwarz criterion	−7.10928	
Log likelihood	35.2876	F-statistic	6.64783	
Durbin-Watson stat	1.825065	Prob (F-statistic)	0.030066	

Data Source Calculated by Eviews5.0 with the data in Table 3

structure of the Pearl River Delta has a positive impact on the GDP growth rate, and the industrial similarity in the Pearl River Delta has led to economic growth. This similarity facilitating economic growth is contrary to the first point of view presented at the beginning of this paper, which repels the "similarity". Then, it is necessary to further analyze the industrial development of the Pearl River Delta, and take the industrial development coordination of the Shenzhen-Dongguan-Huizhou economic circle as an example, which represents the three major economic circles, so as to seek important and valuable information.

3.2   Estimation of the Coordination of Regional Industrial Development

A comprehensive analysis is made on the coordination of industrial development of the three cities from a quantitative perspective. Manufacturing generally has the characteristics of a cross-regional market and a large factor flow, and most of the related sectors are in a perfect competitive state, so it is easy to form isomorphic and homogenous competition. Therefore, manufacturing is the main object of the coordination of Shenzhen, Dongguan and Huizhou, and of this research.[1]

1. Classification of manufacturing activities

In order to highlight the key points and facilitate the analysis, based on the above-mentioned classification criteria for manufacturing, we have selected 21 industries with large proportions, which are divided into four major categories, namely light industry and daily necessities, petrochemical and raw materials, electrical and mechanical equipment, and electronic information, as shown in Table 3. Given the embodiments of intra-industry and intra-product division of labor, the paper estimates and analyzes the variables of the index for industrial similarity, the index for local specialization, industrial capital intensity and capital production efficiency, and builds the up the system for the index of evaluation of the coordination for manufacturing development, as the basis for evaluating the coordination of industrial development in the three regions.

2. Explanation of estimation indexes

(1) Index for industrial similarity

The similarity index refers to the sum of the absolute values of the differences of industrial structure between the two regions. The index is used to examine the degree of regional industrial similarity, and the index values are distributed between 0 and 2. The higher the index value, the higher the degree of industrial difference between the two regions; the lower the index value, the greater the industrial similarity of the two regions. This index measures the degree of similarity or difference in regional industries [15], and can also examine whether regional industries have been assimilated. According to Krugman's method [15], the index equation is as follows:

$$Sjk = \sum_{i=1}^{n} \left| \frac{qij}{qj} - \frac{qik}{qk} \right| \qquad (1)$$

Here, the subscripts j and k represent regions, i represents the industry, q_{ij} and q_{ik} represent the added value of the i industry in the two regions, and q_j and q_k are the total industrial added values of the two regions, respectively.

---

[1] The "industry" in this section refers only to the manufacturing sectors.

Table 3 Classification of the 21 industries involved in the quantitative analysis of industrial coordination

Classification	Manufacturing
Light industry and daily necessities	Processing of food from agricultural products
	Food manufacturing
	Beverage manufacturing
	Textile industry
	Textiles, apparel, footwear, and caps
	Leather, fur, feather and related products
	Furniture manufacturing
	Printing and recording media reproduction
	Cultural, educational and sports goods
	Plastic products
Petrochemical and raw materials	Processing of petroleum, coking, processing of nuclear fuel
	Chemical raw materials and chemical products
	Chemical fibers
	Rubber products
Electrical and mechanical equipment	General purpose machinery
	Special purpose machinery
	Transportation equipment
	Metal products
	Electrical machinery and equipment
	Measuring instruments and machinery for cultural activity and office work
Electronic information	Communication equipment, computers and other electronic equipment

(2) Local Specialization Index

In order to further analyze the differences in the industrial concentration of the three regions, we examine the local specialization index reflecting the degree of industrial agglomeration. The local specialization index refers to the ratio of the proportion of a certain industry in all industries of a certain region to the proportion of the industry in all regions to all its industries of these regions. The index is used to examine trends in the degree of industrial specialization (or concentration) in a region. The smaller the index, the lower the relative concentration of the industry in this region, which means that the level of specialization is low; on the contrary, it indicates that the relative concentration of the industry in this region is high, or the level of specialization is high. If the index value is greater than 1, it indicates that the industrial concentration is higher than the average concentration of other industries in all regions, and hence the specialized concentration of the industry is at a higher position.

The simple model of the regional specialization index is expressed as:

$$Hij = \left| \frac{qij/qi}{\sum qi/Q} \right| \tag{2}$$

Here, the numerator is the ratio of the i industry in the j region to the added value of all industries in the region, and the denominator is the ratio of the i industry in all regions to the added value of all industries.

(3) Index of the estimation of the intensity of industrial capital

The three regions have industrial similarity, but difference in industrial concentration. What are the reasons for the difference? We further analyze the degree of capital intensity. Industrial capital intensity refers to the possession of per capita assets in the corresponding industries. The development of industry generally goes from simple tools to complex equipment, from labor-intensive to capital-intensive. The index reflects the level of investment in industrial equipment, and can also explain the different stages of industrial development, or can show different links of the industrial chain.

(4) Index of the estimation of the ratio of capital output

The capital output ratio refers to the output of industrial added value per unit year-end asset in the corresponding industry. This data reflects the level of capital output. Through the trend of change of the index of the ratio of capital output, we can grasp the growth benefits of the industry in the cities. We calculate the capital output ratio by the industrial added value of the three cities of Shenzhen-Dongguan-Huizhou and the total assets of the industry at the end of the year.

3. Comprehensive evaluation of industrial coordination in the three cities

In the previous section, we analyze the similarity and difference from the four aspects: industrial structure, specialized concentration, capital intensity and capital output ratio and make a detailed analysis of the electronic information industry. Based on the above basic analysis, we classify and merge to form the coefficient of the coordination of industrial development, and construct an index system for the evaluation of the coordination of industrial development to comprehensively evaluate the degree of coordination of industrial development in the three cities.

(1) Index description

The index system can systematically evaluate the degree of coordination of industrial development in relevant regions, and can establish a monitoring system to track the future trends of its coordinated development based on the dynamic changes of data. The larger the index value, the higher the degree of coordination.

For the above-mentioned index of industrial structure, the index o f specialization, that of capital intensity and the ratio of capital output, according to their degree of influence on the industrial coordination of the three cities, we design the weights of 0.25, 0.25, 0.3 and 0.2 respectively. The secondary weights are determined pursuant to the characteristics and importance of industrial development in the three regions. Among them, the commodity index of light industry, the index of electromechanical equipment and that of the electronic information industry of the industrial structure indexes are 0.06, 0.08 and 0.11 respectively, and the like (see Table 4). According to the above weight design, the coefficient of the coordination of industrial development can be obtained for quantitative evaluation and analysis of the status of industrial coordinated development of the three cities.

(2)   Results of the estimation

According to the summary of the various indexes of the three cities and the calculation of the index weighting system of Table 4, the industrial coordination data can be obtained, and the changes in the indexes of the coordination of industrial development of the three cities are shown in Fig. 1.

From Fig. 1, it can be seen that the coefficients of the coordination of industrial development of Shenzhen-Dongguan, Shenzhen-Huizhou and Dongguan-Huizhou show a trend of first decreasing and then increasing. Among them, the coefficients of Shenzhen-Dongguan and Shenzhen-Huizhou have significantly increased since 2009.

Table 4 Design of weights for the indexes of the evaluation of coordination of the industrial development of Shenzhen, Dongguan and Huizhou

Index of industrial division of labor	0.25	Traditional index of light industry	0.06
		Index of electrical and mechanical equipment	0.08
		Index of the electronic information industry	0.11
Index of specialization	0.25	Traditional index of light industry	0.06
		Index of electrical and mechanical equipment	0.08
		Index of the electronic information industry	0.11
Index of capital intensity	0.3	Traditional index of light industry	0.07
		Index of electrical and mechanical equipment	0.10
		Index of the electronic information industry	0.13
Ratio of capital output	0.2	Traditional index of light industry	0.03
		Index of electrical and mechanical equipment	0.07
		Index of the electronic information industry	0.10

Note The secondary indexes are calculated based on the absolute value of the difference between the corresponding industrial indexes of the two cities

Fig. 1 Trends of the coordination of industrial development of Shenzhen, Dongguan and Huizhou from 2004 to 2010

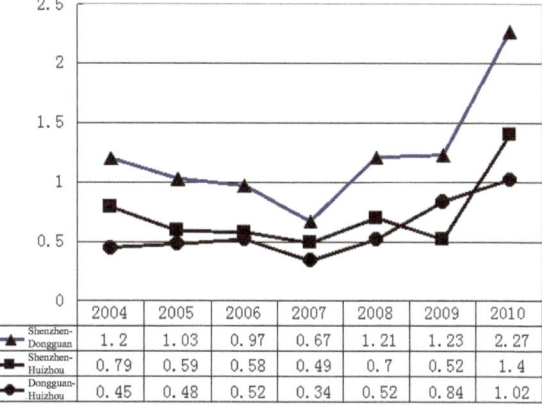

	2004	2005	2006	2007	2008	2009	2010
Shenzhen-Dongguan	1. 2	1. 03	0. 97	0. 67	1. 21	1. 23	2. 27
Shenzhen-Huizhou	0. 79	0. 59	0. 58	0. 49	0. 7	0. 52	1. 4
Dongguan-Huizhou	0. 45	0. 48	0. 52	0. 34	0. 52	0. 84	1. 02

Fig. 2 Trends of coordination of the total manufacturing development of the three cities from 2004 to 2010

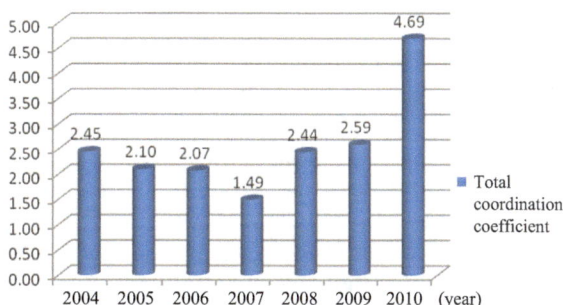

After the integration of the coefficients of the coordination of industrial development among the three cities, we obtain the general industrial coordinated development trends of the three cities from 2004 to 2010 (as shown in Fig. 2).

From Fig. 2, the total coefficient of industrial coordinated development of the three cities dropped from 2.77 in 2004 to 1.49 in 2007, and then rose to 4.69 in 2010. It can be seen that the coordination of the industrial development of the three cities is now on the rise.

3.3   Empirical Conclusions

Considering the statistical dimension, this paper selects the data of the Pearl River Delta for 9 years from 2002 to 2010 and the data of Shenzhen-Dongguan-Huizhou for 7 years from 2004 to 2010 as the research periods, it analyzes the relationship between industrial similarity and economic growth of the Pearl River Delta through the panel data model and the construction of the system of the estimation of the coordination of regional industrial development, and then it estimates the industrial coordination of the development of the manufacturing industry in the three cities of Shenzhen, Dongguan and Huizhou. The following conclusions have been drawn.

First, the coefficient of the similarity of industrial structure of the Pearl River Delta has a positive impact on the growth rate of the GDP. The industrial similarity of the Pearl River Delta has led to economic growth, which is contrary to the attitude of repelling industrial similarity.

Second, with respect to the industrial structure, except for petrochemicals and raw materials, the light industry and daily necessities, electrical and mechanical equipment and electronic information in Shenzhen, Dongguan and Huizhou have a relatively obvious industrial similarity.

Third, regarding the industrial concentration, there are differences among the three cities. The light industry and daily necessities have a high concentration in Dongguan; the petrochemical and raw materials industries have a high concentration in Huizhou; the concentration of the electrical and mechanical equipment industry is relatively high in Dongguan (declining in Dongguan in recent years, while increasing in Shenzhen, and both regions are getting close to each other); the concentration of the electronic information in Shenzhen and Huizhou is relatively high, but relatively low in Dongguan (slightly declining in Huizhou and increasing in Dongguan).

Fourth, in terms of the intensity of industrial capital, the capital intensity of the light industry and daily necessities in Shenzhen, Dongguan and Huizhou is roughly similar. In recent years, the density of industrial capital has improved in the three regions, but it is generally lower than the average level of the whole province. For the electrical and mechanical equipment industry, the capital density is higher in Shenzhen and Huizhou, but lower in Dongguan. The difference of the electronic information industry is obvious, but that of Shenzhen is significantly higher than Huizhou and Dongguan. It can be seen that the electronic information industry in Shenzhen and Dongguan is characterized by differentiated development.

Fifth, from the perspective of the input-output ratio of industrial capital, the light industry, electrical and mechanical equipment and electronic information in Shenzhen, Dongguan and Huizhou have become close to each other (the fluctuations in individual years may be related to large-scale equipment upgrading). Although the models and stages of industrial development of the three regions are different, they also show a consistent developmental trend and the output is averaging, indicating that the models of industrial development of the three regions have their objective reasonableness, and the "invisible hand" of the market plays an effective role.

As stated above, according to the changes in the index of industrial coordination, the degree of coordination of the industrial division of labor of Shenzhen, Dongguan and Huizhou has improved continuously, with the possibility of coordination and construction of super-large industrial clusters. Specifically, first, the three regions have a high degree of industrial similarity in the electrical and mechanical equipment and the electronic information industries, but their internal structures are differentiated. In particular, the three regions have obvious differences in their electronic information industry and there are characteristics of complementary cooperation, so it can be inferred that the electronic information industry has an important trend of forming a large-scale cluster development in Shenzhen, Dongguan and Huizhou. Second, the light industry and daily necessities and the petrochemical and raw material industries have the advantage of specialized agglomerations in Dongguan and Huizhou respectively, and can form light industry clusters and heavy and chemical industry clusters led by Dongguan and Huizhou. Third, productive services are mainly concentrated in Shenzhen. The productive services mainly provide support for industrial development, so a large-scale cluster of productive service industry with Shenzhen as the axis can be formed and radiate over Dongguan and Huizhou.

4 Spatial Layout Strategy of Regional Industries

Considering the above conclusions, taking Shenzhen, Dongguan and Huizhou as an example, in our opinion, it is imperative to promote the division of industrial functions, achieve land-intensive development, and change the old situation of unclear functions and extensive development. By integrating and agglomerating the regional superior resources, the regional industrial layout can be established by strengthening the complementary advantages and a reasonable distribution, with distinctive characteristics, complementary functions and intensive development.

4.1 Clearly Defining the Layout and Orientation of the Functional Areas of the Province

According to the overall layout of areas of industrial functions of Guangdong Province, focusing on the developmental axis of city clusters and the functional orientation of the urban circle on the eastern bank of the Pearl River, with the strategic landscape of "three axes and two belts", we clarify the functions of the various areas and develop the industrial clusters of the three regions, as shown in Fig. 3.

The west axis headed by Qianhai, extends along the Guangzhou-Shenzhen Coastal Expressway, connects to the seaside and riverside areas of Dongguan and docks with the developmental zone of Guangzhou. It is supported by the modern productive services such as port logistics and financial services, accumulates the advantageous traditional light industry and daily necessities through advanced capacity replacement, and forms the developmental axis of a light industry cluster along the eastern bank of the Pearl River. The center axis, relying on the developmental strategy of the Shenzhen-Hong Kong industrial innovation pioneer zone, takes the Shenzhen Dashahe Innovation Corridor as the starting point, runs along the Songshanhu Hightech Zone, is radiated by the advanced manufacturing base in the southern part of Zengcheng, Guangzhou, and extends until Longmen, Huizhou. Supported by the creative services, it will build the large-scale high-end electronic information industry cluster and create an axis of innovative industrial development. The east axis, with

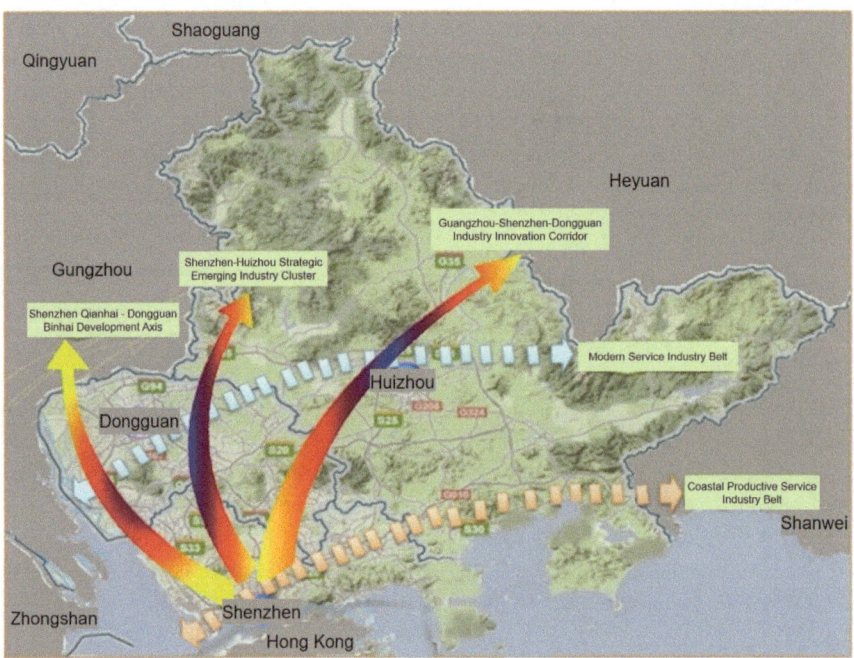

Fig. 3 Developmental axis of city clusters in Guangdong Province

Yantian Port as the window, relies on the "Pingdi-Xinxu-Qingxi" industrial cooperation zone, extends to the Huizhou Zhongkai Economic Development Zone, radiates to the Huidong Industrial Transfer Park, and then echoes with the Shenzhen-Shanwei Industrial Transfer Park and the Heyuan Strategic Emerging Industry Cluster. It forms the industrial cluster led by strategic emerging industries and advanced equipment manufacturing and another cluster dominated by petrochemical raw materials, new energy and new materials. The first belt starts from Qianhaiwan, Yanshekou, Dapengwan in the west, goes to Dayawan in the east and relies on the developed port facilities. It is led by the industries such as finance, logistics and specialized services, forms the industrial cluster of modern productive services and provides strong support for the manufacturing industrial cluster. The second belt starts from the inland river port of the Pearl River in Dongguan, converges with Songhanhu along Guancheng, and runs to Huidong, Huizhou in the east. Based on the relatively abundant developmental factor resources around the axis, it makes full use of the favorable conditions of adjoining port productive services, the resource of a consumption population in Dongguan and the unique tourism resource of Huizhou and builds the industrial cluster belt of characteristic services. Clearly defining the developmental strategy of the city clusters of our province is crucial for the spatial layout of the three cities for coordinated industrial development.

4.2 The Strategy of Industrial Spatial Layout of Shenzhen-Dongguan-Huizhou

According to the developmental strategy of city clusters in our province, we should plan the layout of industrial development of Shenzhen, Dongguan and Huizhou according to the characteristics of the above analysis. The industrial developmental layout is shown in Fig. 4.

According to the above-mentioned layout of industrial development, the construction of industrial cluster developmental carriers has improved. By 2015, four industrial clusters had been built around the three axes and two belts. First, to accelerate the construction of the Dongguan (Huidong) and Dongguan (Huizhou) industrial transfer parks. It is docked with Dongguan's industrial transfer and forms a new base for the development of light industry and daily necessities. Second, to launch the "Dayawan-Pingshan" demonstration zone for the cooperation on the new energy industry led by Huizhou, smoothen the upstream and downstream nodes of the petrochemical industry to construct the new clusters of energy (including petroleum, electric power, new energy) and the chemical industry, and form an industrial cluster base with a large output value and scale. Third, with the "Pingdi-Xinxu-Qingxi" industrial cooperation zone as the carrier, to form the new industrial cluster bases of electronic information and electrical and mechanical equipment. Fourth, to promote the construction of the Shenzhen-Shanwei economic cooperation zone. It will

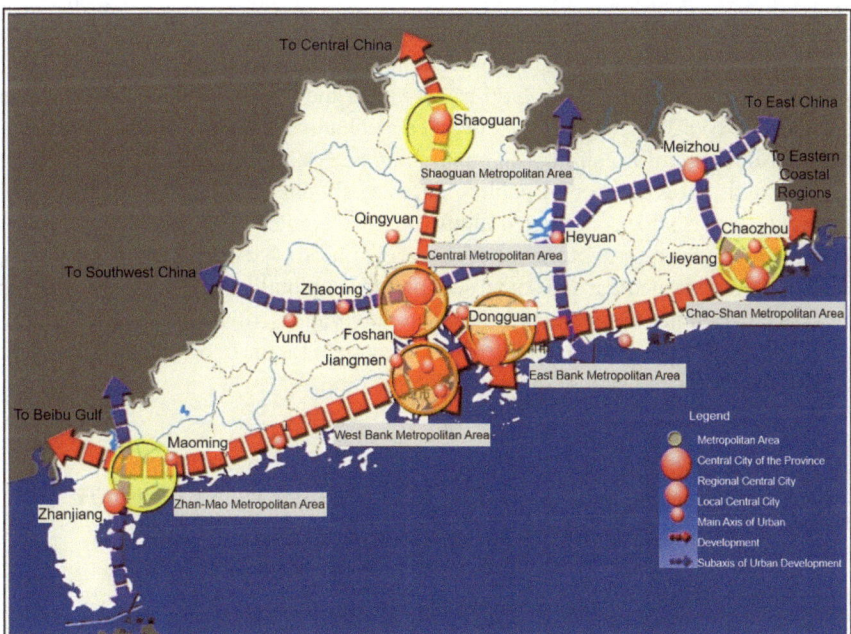

Fig. 4 The layout of industrial development of Shenzhen-Dongguan-Huizhou

be built into the base of strategic emerging industrial clusters such as the high-end electronic information industry.

5 Policy Suggestions

An institutional environment conducive to coordinated industrial development must be created according to the key tasks and the construction of an industrial cluster base for the coordinated development of the three regions.

5.1 Bringing About Innovations to the Institutional Mechanism Conducive to Coordinated Industrial Development

The existing administrative system constraints must be broken. The office for the coordination of the Shenzhen-Dongguan-Huizhou industry policy must be established to plan industrial construction in the economic circle from a strategic perspective, coordinate and unify the specialized industrial planning of the three regions, build a long-term mechanism for coordinated and sustainable industrial development, improve the mechanisms of regular meetings and coordination between senior leadership and departments, coordinate inter-regional interests and eliminate administrative divisions and obstacles. The government evaluation system must be changed. A statistical indicator system should be set up for the three regions with evaluation indicators of coordinated development and a mechanism for the disclosure of industrial coordination information. The public finance system of the three regions must be innovated and a number of public platforms should be constructed and shared to provide services for coordinated industrial development. They should strengthen coordination in the reform of the household registration system, employment system, education system, medical and social security system, build a unified framework for the system of human resources flow, achieve integration within the regional framework, and create a favorable institutional environment for the integrated development of the Shenzhen-Dongguan-Huizhou economic circle.

5.2 Coordinating and Securing Factor Resources Conducive to the Construction of an Industrial Cluster

Importance should be given to strengthening the cooperation of financial sectors of the three regions, giving full play to the role of finance in nourishing the manufacturing industry, establishing a cooperation and exchange mechanism between financial departments and financial regulatory authorities and regularly researching and consulting on financial cooperation issues of common concern. The three cities should jointly hold financial negotiation activities, organize banks, venture capitals and credit guarantee institutions to dock with small and medium-sized enterprises, support the branch establishment of financial institutions, expand business to other regions, jointly build financing platforms for enterprises and promote the transition of the inter-regional transfer payment system to the unified settlement system. Logistics cooperation should be accelerated to improve the efficiency and level of logistics services, promote the unified logistics export regulations, establish the customs regulations of bonded warehouses, achieve low-cost rapid customs clearance, and reduce the logistics costs of enterprises. The three cities should coordinate the mechanism for the allocation of energy and water resources for industrial development, promote cooperation in the field of energy and water conservation construction projects and secure the supply of high-quality, efficient and clean energy needed for the development of industrial clusters. The land use model for industrial development must be optimized and the "double transfer" strategy must be actively implemented to coordinate the land resource complementarity for the construction of industrial clusters by means of the development and utilization of marginal land resources and "vacating the cage to change birds".

5.3 Creating a Business Environment Conducive to the Construction of an Industrial Cluster

They should strive to build an international business environment that is rule of law, efficient, creditworthy, fair and just. The three regions must promote the innovation of the commercial system, accelerate the reform of the administrative examination and approval system, streamline the business registration formalities, explore the regional company registration system, allow the use of "Guangdong" in the name of cross-regional large groups, and develop a batch of cross-regional large-scale groups in the fields of industry, commerce, foreign trade, finance, tourism, education and culture, and information, so that the coordinated development of regional industries becomes an operation within enterprise groups in a certain sense and facilitates the construction of cross-regional industrial clusters. The unified local brand trademark must be established to promote the joint development of cross-regional common brands and improve the visibility and competitiveness of the clusters. They should actively advance the construction of a credit system, enhance the protection of intellectual property rights, break the constraints of local policies through regional agreements, regional conventions or partial consultations, multi-party agreements, etc., create an environment of fair market competition, and build a large regional market. A world-class international business environment and a high-quality cultural life circle must be constructed to attract the world's emerging industries and multinational company headquarters to join the cluster development.

5.4 Building a Public Platform Conducive to Enhancing the Capabilities for Technology Innovation

The three regions should make full use of their respective advantages of innovation resources to create a number of innovative public platforms. They should bring about innovations to the mechanism of linking industries, universities and research, promote the healthy development of the industrial alliance, attract more local enterprises, universities and scientific research institutions to enter the industrial alliance, and create a good atmosphere for regional cooperation and exchange. For the key industrial clusters in the three regions, the world-class high-tech talents and scientific research institutions should be introduced through public platforms. Attention should be paid to a number of common scientific and technological resources, which may be arranged by uniform financial coordination to solve the issues of key common technology research and development and conversion of application results, and jointly develop key technologies in a number of key areas. Shenzhen must give full play to its role of industrial developmental incubator, improve the investment environment, introduce design, brand, accounting, law, exhibition and other professional services from Hong Kong, radiate the manufacturing sectors of the three regions and enhance the competitiveness of the industrial clusters.

The coordinated industrial development and spatial layout of Shenzhen-Dongguan-Huizhou is representative of the Pearl River Delta. Through in-depth research, it has been found that a lot of viewpoints proposed in the past are not clear or wrong. Do the same problems exist in other economic circles such as Zhuhai-Zhongshan-Jiangmen and Guangzhou-Foshan-Zhaoqing? This needs further research to clarify. However, one point is definite: Today the domestic and international economic landscape is undergoing tremendous changes, so it is possible for there to be paths to regional economic growth that can generate the sustainable endogenous driving force, namely accelerating the inter-regional industrial division of labor and trade, advancing their coordinated development and the reasonable layout of inter-regional industries.

References

1. Weng Jichuan, An Analysis on Assimilated Industrial Structures in the Pearl River Delta, *World Regional Studies*, 2006(1).
2. Yang Yongfu, The Change of Governmental Functions: the Crux in the Economic Integration of the Pearl River Delta Area, *Academic Research*, 2009(8).
3. Martin, R., and Sunley, P. Paul Krugman's Geographical Economics and its Implications for Regional Development Theory: A Critical Assessment. Economic Geography, 1996, 72, (3).
4. Michael E. Porter, *The Competitive Advantage of Nations*, Beijing: Huaxia Publishing House, 2000, pp. 15–22.
5. Porter, M.E. (1998). Cluster and New Economics of Competition, Harvard Business Review 11.
6. Yang Xiaokai, *Principles of Economics*, Beijing: China Social Sciences Press, 1998.

7. Yang Xiaokai, *New Classical Economics and Inframarginal Analysis*, China Renmin University Press, 2000.
8. Yang Kaizhong, *Towards Space Integration – China's Market Economy and Regional Development Strategy*, Chengdu: Sichuan People's Publishing House, 1993.
9. Isard, W. Further thoughts on future directions for regional science [M]. M.I.T. Press, 1999.
10. Fujita. Remarks on the general theory of location and space-economy [J]. Annals of Regional Science, 1999, 33: 383–388.
11. Ohlin, Bertli, Interregional and Inter-national Trade [M], Cambridge, MA: Harvard University Press, 1933.
12. Krugman P. Scale Economies, Product Differentiation, and the Pattern of Trade [J]. American Economic Review, 1980, (70): 950–959.
13. Krugman, P. Increasing Returns and Economic Geography [J]. Journal of Development Economics, 1991a, 49 (1): 137–150.
14. Venables, A. Equilibrium Locations of Vertically Linked Industries [J]. International Economic Review, 1996, 37 (2): 341–359.
15. Krugman, P. Geography and Trade [M], MIT Press, Cambridge, MA, 1991b.

Liu Jing Ph.D. of Institute of Hong Kong, Macao & SEZs Economy, Jinan University, and Economist of Guangdong Institute of Industry Development, with research interests in regional economy, SEZ economy and Hong Kong-Macao-Pearl River Delta economy.

Chapter 11
A Study on the Structural Functions and Management System for the Integrated Development of the Pearl River East Bank Metropolitan Area (II)

Nie Xinping

Abstract This paper puts forward the necessity of regional cooperation for the industrial integration and institutional innovation of Shenzhen, Dongguan and Huizhou. Then, the structural functions for the integration of the Pearl River East Bank Metropolitan Area are studied from three aspects: the integration of economic development, that of social services and that of environmental governance. Next, the system for the management of the integration of the Pearl River East Bank Metropolitan Area is studied in terms of the improvement of the mechanism of interest sharing and distribution for integration, for the structure of regional cooperation and for the system of cross-regional governance. Finally, policy suggestions are given on structural functions and the system of management for integrated development of the metropolitan area.

Keywords Integration of the Pearl River East Bank Metropolitan Area · Structural functions · System of management

1 Research Question

Shenzhen, Dongguan and Huizhou, if these three cities want to catch up with and surpass famous international city clusters and become a world-class metropolitan area with strong international competitiveness and an extensive radiation force, they have to profoundly integrate their industry, expand and strengthen their regional industrial chain, occupy the global high-end of the industrial chain, promote the competitiveness of regional industry and enhance the degree of integration of social services and environmental governance.

Promoting the integration of the Pearl River East Bank Metropolitan Area (PREBMA) has a better basis for cooperation and more urgent needs than regional

N. Xinping (✉)
Shenzhen Municipal People's Government, Shenzhen 518000, China
e-mail: ccsezr@szu.edu.cn

© Social Sciences Academic Press 2020
Y. Yuan (ed.), *Studies on China's Special Economic Zones 3*,
Research Series on the Chinese Dream and China's Development Path,
https://doi.org/10.1007/978-981-13-9841-4_11

cooperation in other parts of the country, so it should really make a difference. The Shenzhen Special Economic Zone, with the new mission, should go hand in hand with Dongguan and Huizhou to advance regional cooperation, implement institutional innovation, explore the experience of effective cross-regional governance, provide demonstrations for facilitating regional cooperation in China, and find a far-reaching path for regional development.

2 Structural Functions for the Integration of the Pearl River East Bank Metropolitan Area

2.1 Economic Developmental Integration

1. Increasing integration of the three cities and enhancing the regional industrial chains

The industrial chain distributed in the integrated economic circle is not only the real subject of regional economic competition, but also the key force that determines regional competitiveness, especially the core competitiveness. For example, the automobile industrial chain in Detroit and the IC and PC industrial chain in Taiwan. The development of these regional industrial chains shows that the scale and specialization effects of regional industrial chains can reduce the cost of industrial development, enhance the industrial competitiveness of the entire region, and create conditions for industrial internationalization. In order to enhance industrial competitiveness and radiation, the three cities, Shenzhen, Dongguan and Huizhou, must increase the integration of their industrial chains and enhance several regional industrial chains.

2. Strengthening industrial cooperation in border areas and providing new space for industrial development

If Shenzhen, Dongguan and Huizhou are viewed separately, the border areas of the three cities are far away from the central areas. If they are viewed as a whole, the border areas are the central areas of the three cities, thus having an important strategic position for development. The border areas of the three cities are relatively backward in development, but the available land is relatively abundant, and they are situated at very important central positions in the transfer of the industrial gradient of Shenzhen, Dongguan and Huizhou and provide new spaces for the industrial cooperation of the three cities. Therefore, the three cities vigorously promote the development of their border areas, and through the establishment of a cross-border industrial cooperation demonstration zone and other means, actively build the belt of development of the border industry and create new growth engines for the economic growth of the three cities.

3. Enhancing industrial cooperation of Shenzhen-Huizhou and guiding industrial transfer in an orderly manner

With the increasingly scarce space for land development space in recent years, the rising price of factors, and the impact of the RMB appreciation and the promulgation of the new labor law, the production and operation costs of enterprises have gradually increased, and the space for development of Shenzhen's enterprises has been further squeezed. Faced with big development bottlenecks, many enterprises choose to move to other regions. Huizhou is relatively backward in development and has ample land spaces for development. By virtue of its advantages in location, transportation and labor costs, Huizhou has attracted quite a number of enterprises from Shenzhen. Driven by the promotion of the dual transfer of industry and labor, and the acceleration of the transformation of the model of economic development, the industrial transfer from Shenzhen to Huizhou has become an irresistible trend. However, the spontaneous movement of enterprises on the market basis and the transfer of enterprises led by industrial associations are obviously disordered, and it is difficult to form industrial clusters and obtain strong industrial support. Shenzhen-Huizhou cooperation is the key point of industrial cooperation in the Pearl River East Bank region. In order to boost the industrial cooperation and development and guide the orderly transfer of enterprises, the two cities must cooperate on the construction of industrial parks in Huizhou and jointly build "Songshanhu" of Huizhou.

4. Coordinating the layout of industrial development and building the industrial developmental axis of Shenzhen, Dongguan and Huizhou

In the industrial development planning of Shenzhen, Dongguan and Huizhou, Shenzhen mainly constructs and perfects the "one belt, four zones and nine bases" as well as high-end service function zones. "One belt" refers to the high-tech industrial belt. "Four zones" refer to the four major industrial function zones, including the core technology function zone, the western high-tech industrial function zone, the middle high-tech industrial function zone and the east advanced manufacturing function zone. "Nine bases" refer to nine industrial bases. The high-end service industrial function zones refer to the important high-end service projects, including the Qianhai Shenzhen-Hong Kong Modern Service Industry Cooperation Zone, the Futian Finance Center, the Caiwuwei Financial Center Zone, the Nanshan Financial and Business District, the Longgang Financial Service Base and the Sungang Logistics Headquarter Base.

2.2 Social Service Integration

1. Integration of basic public services

The integration of basic public services in the three cities can facilitate the free movement of labor within the region, which will greatly support the free movement of capital, technology, information and other factors of production, help to further improve institutional arrangements for the supply of public services of people's livelihood, largely ameliorate the overall level of welfare of the region and expand the space for social development of the three cities.

According to the results of the questionnaire survey conducted by the research team for residents of Shenzhen, Dongguan and Huizhou, in terms of the "most urgent needs for integration of Shenzhen, Dongguan and Huizhou", 34.1% of the respondents considered "cooperation on education, medical care and other fields regarding the people's livelihood" are the most urgent need ranking in first place; followed by the "docking of transportation infrastructure"; and then "public security cooperation", which was selected by 15.8% of the respondents. Through the interactive analysis of the respondents' places of residence, the respondents in these cities have basically consistent opinions on the most urgent needs for integration. For "cooperation on education, medical care and other fields regarding the people's livelihood", the proportion is 36.4% for Shenzhen, 32.8% for Dongguan and 33.9% for Huizhou, all of which rank top. Therefore, the integration of the three cities has the most urgent needs for public services, such as education, medical care, employment and public security, which are the urgent tasks faced by the local governments of the three cities, see Table 1 for detail.

2. Infrastructure integration

At the forefront of China's reform and opening-up, the Shenzhen, Dongguan and Huizhou region has achieved the leap-forward improvement of infrastructure after more than 30 years of large-scale construction, thus providing a solid foundation for supporting and leading the regional economic and social development. However, due to the different interests of various parties and the inconsistency of institutional mechanisms, the link of infrastructure and resources of the three cities cannot satisfy the requirements for regional integration. Strengthening the construction and docking

Table 1 Most urgent needs for integration in the mind of the respondents of Shenzhen, Dongguan and Huizhou

	Industrial cooperation (%)	Cooperation on education, medical care and other fields regarding the people's livelihood (%)	Environmental protection and ecological governance (%)	Docking of transportation infrastructure (%)	Public security cooperation (%)	Others (%)
Shenzhen	16.8	36.4	7.5	26.8	11.8	0.7
Dongguan	11.7	32.8	13.3	19.4	22.2	0.6
Huizhou	16.1	33.9	16.1	18.3	15.6	–
Other	16.4	28.4	14.9	23.9	16.4	–

Data Source Public Willingness Survey Report for the Integration of Shenzhen, Dongguan and Huizhou

of infrastructure such as transportation, energy and water resources is important for promoting and supporting the economic integration of the three cities, expanding the space for urban and industrial development, and building the international and urbanized Shenzhen, Dongguan and Huizhou economic circle.

3. Integration of service development

An important symbol of the formation of city clusters is a central city with strong economic strength. The central city is at the core and in the dominant position of the city cluster and plays an organizational and leading role in the overall regional social and economic activities. To push forward the integration of Shenzhen, Dongguan and Huizhou, the central city must enhance its capabilities for factor concentration and economic radiation, strengthen its urban functions and expand its space for services. To "connect Hong Kong and serve Dongguan and Huizhou", on the one hand, it should give full play to the role of Hong Kong as a world-leading city, and on the other hand, Shenzhen must be vigorously strengthened as a core and hub central city to serve the surrounding areas through radiation of the service sectors, improvement of the functions of headquarters and the control of important strategic resources such as airports and terminals.

2.3 Integration of Environmental Governance

Wang [1] pointed out that the purposes of environmental management in the metropolitan area were to solve the problems of environmental pollution and ecological damage caused by the regional economic or social activities, ensure the security of the regional environment in the metropolitan area and achieve sustainable development. Among the three cities, Shenzhen realizes the best economic development and the fastest speed of development, so it should take greater responsibility in controlling the environmental pollution and play a leading role in the management of the ecological environment and the construction of the ecological pattern. Dongguan and Huizhou should also strengthen their environmental protection by the internationally accepted principle of "whoever pollutes, pays", actively carry out the cross-border river pollution treatment, disposal of solid wastes and construction of ecological corridors as well as jointly building a green and high-quality living circle of Shenzhen, Dongguan and Huizhou.

3 The System of Management for the Integration of the Pearl River East Bank Metropolitan Area

3.1 Improving the Mechanism of Interest Sharing and Distribution for the Integration of Shenzhen, Dongguan and Huizhou

The integration of Shenzhen, Dongguan and Huizhou involves the interest game of a multitude of entities, including higher-level governments, municipal governments of the three cities and enterprises as the mainstay of the market economy. The key is the interest mechanism of cooperation. The three cities should improve the interest incentive and distribution mechanism for cooperation, build a reasonable coordination of interests, benefit sharing and an interest compensation mechanism and avoid the loss of overall efficiency due to internal conflicts.

3.2 Optimizing the Regional Structure of Cooperation and Exploring the Institutional Mechanism of Cross-Regional Governance

1. Setting up the Shenzhen, Dongguan and Huizhou Committee for the Promotion of Integration

The current joint conference system of the Party and the administration of Shenzhen-Dongguan-Huizhou is upgraded until the Shenzhen, Dongguan and Huizhou Integration Promotion Committee is established to seek an effective means of transcending the "economy of administrative areas". In order to promote the integration of Shenzhen, Dongguan and Huizhou, the three cities can refer to the theory of new regionalism, aim to reduce administrative barriers, attempt to build the cross-regional governance system, advance the management of regional government to regional governance, proceed from urban internal management to cross-region joined-up management, and replace the traditional top-down command-driven system with participatory governance.

2. Establishing the Shenzhen, Dongguan and Huizhou Center for the Promotion of Integration

The administrative organizations have been established for cooperation and the Shenzhen, Dongguan and Huizhou Center for the Promotion of Integration was set up. The functions and responsibilities have been clarified for the joint conference system of the Party and the administration and the regular meeting of deputy mayors of the three cities, the staffing and arrangements of functional divisions for cooperation have been improved within the general governmental offices or development and reform commissions of the three cities. When necessary, the Shenzhen, Dongguan and Huizhou Center for the Promotion of Integration may be established tentatively.

3. Creating the Shenzhen, Dongguan and Huizhou Committee for Overseeing and Evaluating Integration

The main duties of the Shenzhen, Dongguan and Huizhou Committee for Overseeing and Evaluating Integration are overseeing and evaluating the execution of the three cities' integrated decision-making, so that it is specific, their work objectives, progress, laws, performance and economic aspects of the cooperation, so as to make sure of its excellent execution, that it meets the expectations and also evaluates the effectiveness.

4 Conclusions and Policy Suggestions

4.1 Conclusions of the Research

The basic framework for the integrated development of the metropolitan area includes three dimensions: spatial expansion, structural functions and management system. Spatial expansion is the result of integrated development, expands the space for economic development, opens up virtual developmental space, and builds an open and international metropolitan area; the structural functions of the metropolitan area are similar to the economic, social, and environmental functions of all administrative bodies, which establish a unified market through industrial cooperation, give play to the role of economic integration, promote the reform of the administrative system, and achieve major breakthroughs in public services, infrastructure, and social security. Finally, it builds up the mechanism of competition and cooperation, and formulates policies of integration such as setting up the organizations for the management of development, transforming governmental functions, giving play to the role of enterprises, and establishing a benefit-sharing mechanism to form a synergy of integration.

4.2 Policy Suggestions for the Structural Functions for the Integration of the Pearl River East Bank Metropolitan Area

1. Industrial cooperation, unified market system

The development of economic integration is driven by industrial cooperation. The three cities need to strengthen their efforts at industrial cooperation, innovate their model of industrial cooperation, integrate industrial chains, jointly establish the demonstration zone for cooperation on border industries, and create the three-city industrial development axis, so that they can further optimize the allocation of regional industrial resources and expand the space for industrial development. They should establish unified and open markets for products, technologies, property rights and talents, unified technical standards, market entry and mutual quality recognition system, as well as a unified information-sharing platform. The fair and unified market entry conditions should be implemented in the cooperation zone for the products and enterprises of the three cities, which should enjoy equal treatment in business registration, administrative approval, and tax levying and management.

2. The construction of infrastructures

Well-developed urban traffic is an important condition for the integrated development of the metropolitan area. By establishing a perfect transportation system such as "one-hour" living circle and bus integration, the three cities can reduce the costs of circulation and operations for the people, logistics and information flow, accelerate the integration of regional resources, and improve the overall image and operational efficiency of the region. Shenzhen, as the central city of the East Bank Metropolitan Area, should have the infrastructure corresponding to its role, construct a safe and stable energy supply system and support the integrated development of the metropolitan area. Strengthening the construction of infrastructures of the metropolitan area requires the cooperation of local governments at all levels. Related problems must be solved under the principle of mutual benefit and a win-win outcome. Moreover, the integrated construction of infrastructures needs to be vigorously supported by capitals, needs to improve the investment and financing model, and do well in the financial guarantee for the construction of infrastructures.

4.3 Policy Suggestions for the System of Management for the Integration of the Pearl River East Bank Metropolitan Area

1. Intensifying the reform of the system and transfer of government functions

The integration of the metropolitan area aims to break the shackles of the economy of administrative regions. According to China's national conditions, the integrated development of metropolitan areas requires the reform of the political system, especially a profound reform of the system of the evaluation of the performance of the government. Integrated development needs government dominance and market operations. The government should play a leading role in the integrated development of metropolitan areas. The government must respect the laws of the market and strive to enable the market mechanism to play a fundamental role in the formation of the metropolitan area. At the same time, it must also establish a streamlined and efficient cooperative system of management, actively promote the socialization and marketization of the development and operation of the cooperative demonstration zone, and accelerate the formation of a government-led, market-operating and industry-coordinated scientific development landscape.

2. Establishing a mechanism for the distribution of interests

A metropolitan area involves different administrative regions. As a result, the biggest problem faced by the integration of the metropolitan area is the coordination of interests among the regions. Moreover, the metropolitan area involves different stakeholders. Hence, the mechanism for the distribution of interests is an important guarantee for the success of regional cooperation. The East Bank Metropolitan Area should uphold the principle of joint responsibility and interest sharing, and establish a reasonable mechanism for the distribution of interests. The distribution of interests must consider the current economic benefits, and also the distribution of economic benefits in future cooperation, and the balance of regional economic and social development, so as to allow for long-term effective regional cooperation, arouse the enthusiasm for cooperation of the three cities and ensure sustainable development of regional cooperation.

References

1. Wang Fanghua, Chen Hongmin, *Research on the Development and Management of Metropolitan Regions* [M], Shanghai: SDX Joint Publishing Company, 2007.

Nie Xinping Director of the Development and Reform Commission of Shenzhen.

Chapter 12
The Development of China's Special Economic Zones and Poverty Reduction—Overview of the Seminar on China-Africa Poverty Reduction and Development

Zhang Ping

Abstract The experience of the special economic zones is summarized with consideration to the actual situations in Africa: the development of agriculture with a view to promoting industrialization, the industrialization driven by exports, the establishment of cooperation between domestic and foreign capitals, the development of private sectors, no government interference in the investment field, and the offer of preferential policies and an environment for the industrial development of enterprises.

Keywords China's special economic zones · Developmental line of thought · Poverty reduction

1 About the Seminar

The China-Africa Poverty Reduction and Development Seminar was held at Shenzhen University from January 9th to 13th, 2012. It was co-hosted by the International Poverty Reduction Center in China (IPRCC) and the United Nations Development Program (UNDP), organized by the China Center for Special Economic Zone Research of Shenzhen University and received support from the Shenzhen Municipal Counterpart Poverty Reduction Office. More than 50 government officials, experts, scholars, representatives of international organizations and entrepreneurs from China and six African countries gathered together and had a discussion about the issue of China's SEZs and Poverty Reduction. Mr. Zheng Wenkai, Deputy Director of the State Council Leading Group Office of Poverty Alleviation and Development, Hailemeskel Tefera, State Minister of the Ministry of Urban Development and Construction of Ethiopia, Tao Yitao, Deputy Secretary and Director of the China Center for Special Economic Zone Research of Shenzhen University, Mr. Christophe Bahuet,

Z. Ping (✉)
Shenzhen University, Shenzhen, China
e-mail: pzhng@163.com

© Social Sciences Academic Press 2020
Y. Yuan (ed.), *Studies on China's Special Economic Zones 3*,
Research Series on the Chinese Dream and China's Development Path,
https://doi.org/10.1007/978-981-13-9841-4_12

UNDP China Country Director, and Ms. Liu Jin, Vice Chairperson of the Shenzhen Municipal Science, Industry, Trade and Information Commission addressed the opening ceremony.

This seminar is the continuation of the conference on China-Africa Poverty Reduction and Development held in Ethiopia in 2010. It aims to provide attendees with an opportunity to meet face-to-face to discuss policies, strategic and technical issues related to the development and implementation of the special economic zones and the growth of competitive industrial clusters. Furthermore, attendees also paid a visit to famous enterprises such as Huawei, ZTE and Tencent and listened to the introduction.

Representatives of African countries attending the seminar included Amare Asgedom, Head of the Housing Development and Government Building Construction Bureau, Ministry of Urban Development and Construction, Ethiopia; Kalu Kebede, Engineering Director of the Ethiopian Leather Industry Development Institute; Bekele Gebre Ftago, Deputy Director of the Development Bank of Ethiopia and Addis Ababa Land Development and Urban Renewal Agency; Pre Simféitchéou, Chief of Staff and Chief Economist, Office of the Prime Minister, Togo; Mawussi Djossou SEMODJI, Director of the Cabinet and Economist, Ministry of Economy and Finance, Togo; Simão Joaquim, Head of the Special Economic Zones Office, Ministry of Planning and Development, Mozambique; Ouchar HISSEINE, Head of the Department of Industry and Small Enterprises, Ministry of Trade, Industry and Small Enterprises, Chad; Mugo KIBATI, Director General of Kenya Vision 2030 Delivery Secretariat; AFLA A. GHEBREHIWET, Official of the Department of Millennium Development Goals Tracking and Reporting, Ministry of National Development, Eritrea; Rosine MAWANGA, Director General of the Social Economy, Ministry of SMEs and Crafts, Gabon; BASSEY AKPANYUNG, Director of the Department of International Cooperation, National Planning Commission, Nigeria; and Cosmas Mbambe, Principal Economist, Ministry of Finance, Zimbabwe.

Chinese officials also participated in the discussions and summary, including Huang Chengwei and He Xiaojun, deputy directors of the International Poverty Reduction Center in China; Counselor Lu Huiying, the Department of African Affairs of the Ministry of Foreign Affairs of China; Steven Sabey, Senior Policy Adviser of UNDP in China; Chen Song, Director of the Policy Planning Division, Department of Policy Planning, Ministry of Foreign Affairs of China; Jin Baisong, Deputy Director of the Department of Foreign Economy and Trade, Chinese Academy of International Trade and Economic Cooperation, Ministry of Commerce (MOFCOM); Bai Chengyu, Division Director, China International Center for Economic and Technical Exchanges, MOFCOM; Chen Xin, Head of the Management Division, Suzhou Branch of the China Development Bank; Yu Yangang, Head of Economic Research Division, Policy Research Office of Shenzhen; and Director Liu Yigang and Deputy Director Xu Jianming, Shenzhen Municipal Counterpart Poverty Reduction Office.

Participating representative experts included Professor Li Xiaoyun, Dean of the College of Humanities and Development Studies, China Agricultural University; Wan Zengwei, President of the Shanghai Pudong Institute of Reform and Development; Zhang Yansheng, Researcher of the Institute of Foreign Economy of the National Development and Reform Commission (NDRC); and famous scholars such as Tao Yitao, Yuan Yiming, Cao Longqi, Gao Xingmin and Zhong Ruoyu from the China Center for Special Economic Zone Research, Shenzhen University.

2 Important Speeches and Comments

This seminar aimed to explore the ways in which African countries can learn from China's experiences in economic development and investment policies in the process of accelerating economic and social development, reducing poverty and promoting the Millennium Development Goals. China shared extensive and in-depth experience in policy, institutions, public-private partnerships and technical issues with African countries. The implementation of special economic zones, industrial development from planning and design to management operations, as well as the experience of attracting private investment under the regulatory and corporate environment provided the main materials for the discussions.

Mr. Zheng Wenkai said in his speech that in China's thirty years of the process of economic growth and poverty reduction, the Special Economic Zones (SEZs) have been undertaking the important mission of institutional reform, technical advancement, and S&T innovation. SEZs have not only rapidly developed into new growth poles which produced large numbers of new talents, but also played an irreplaceable role in extending its new experience in driving the developmental process of the rest of China. He pointed out that China is willing to share its experience gained in the process of poverty reduction and development with the other developing countries, African countries in particular, and would like very much to continue its learning from other countries as well. China will actively promote international cooperation and exchanges in the field of poverty reduction to jointly make China and African countries stronger and more prosperous.

In his speech, Mr. Christophe Bahuet, UNDP China Country Director pointed out that, as pioneers of the implementation of China's policies of opening up and economic transformation, SEZs' development cannot be separated from the big environment and the support of national macroeconomic policies. They have accumulated experience and lessons in aspects such as macroeconomic policies, industrial strategies, employment creation, and the relevant mechanisms to cope with challenges, which can provide reference to other developing countries.

Huang Chengwei, Deputy Director of the International Center for Poverty Reduction in China, commented on the relationship between special economic zones and poverty alleviation: the special economic zone was a special development model adopted by China in the process of reform and opening-up and accelerating development. The core element for the special economic zone was doing experiments of various policies in a region in an innovative way, forming an intensifying effect, and driving the economic development of surrounding areas and the country by diffusion. The development in the past three decades proved that this model was an effective developmental model in the process of economic and social development. Today, this model had a positive effect on the poverty-stricken areas and population.

3   Overview of Expert Opinions

This meeting arranged a number of expert seminars. Experts and representatives discussed how African countries could learn from China's experience of developing special economic zones and achieving sustainable poverty reduction and promote their own development and poverty reduction from the perspectives and levels of strategies, policies, country cases and industrial development.

Professor Tao Yitao, Deputy Secretary of Shenzhen University and Director of the China Center for Special Economic Zone Research, explained the theory of "Special Economic Zones and China's Path". She pointed out that the institutional changes in the Chinese society with the establishment of the market economy as the main aspect constituted a difficult and splendid course for the growth and development of special economic zones. In a broader sense, especially for the traditional system and developmental model of the period of the planned economy, the establishment of special economic zones was a key choice for scientific development, which opened the way for the scientific development of the Chinese society. When people's economic value increased, our society would have some new and better opportunities. The government should not lead the social economy in wishful thinking. Instead, it should create an institutional environment while respecting the market, complete the supply of public goods, and build social welfare mechanisms. Without the reform of the political system that was compatible with the economic system, the reform of the economic system could not be truly successful.

Professor Yuan Yiming, Deputy Director of the China Center for Special Economic Zone Research, Shenzhen University, first analyzed the contribution of China's economic growth to poverty reduction in the past 30 years from a macroscopic perspective, and then explained the internal mechanism of the positive role of FDI and non-FDI on poverty reduction through an empirical research of special economic zones. Finally, according to the different paths for the effect of foreign investment on poverty reduction in the different periods of special economic zone development, several constructive and actionable suggestions for African countries' poverty reduction strategies were proposed.

Zhang Yansheng, Researcher from the Institute of Foreign Economy of the National Development and Reform Commission, focused on the reason for great achievements of the reform and opening-up—the development of a market economy, and the government's push for the establishment and new changes of special economic zones, which enabled the SEZ to become a window and bridge for the development of the market economy. The role of window and bridge allowed for China to be actively integrated into the global collaborative production and further accomplish the economic takeoff of China. Then, Professor Zhang Yansheng indicated that only by active strategic adjustment and institutional innovation could the existing problems be solved.

Yu Yangang, Head of the Economic Research Division, Policy Research Office of Shenzhen, reviewed the 30-year history of Shenzhen as a special economic zone in the report "Sustainable Development as the Absolute Principle—Some Practical

Explorations of the Rapid Development of the Shenzhen Special Economic Zone to Prosperity", and summarized the four positive practices of Shenzhen for its rapid development towards prosperity: first, always adhering to development as the top priority and growing to be an important economic center city in the country; second, unwaveringly insisting on the reform, and becoming the pioneering area of institutional innovation; third, adhering to the path of external development and actively integrating into economic globalization; and fourth, insisting that science and technology is the primary productive force and its becoming the first national innovative city.

Mr. Pre Simféitchéou, Chief of Staff and Chief Economist at the Office of the Prime Minister of Togo, gave a brief introduction to Togo's current poverty reduction strategies. First, the government regulation was enhanced to lay the foundation for poverty reduction strategies; then, the structural economic reform was strengthened and the business model was improved to ensure sustainable economic growth; the human capital in Togo was developed from the perspective of education and medical care; and finally, the gap among regions was narrowed through the construction of infrastructures. These were four key points for the current poverty reduction strategies of Togo.

Mr. BASSEY AKPANYUNG, Director of the Department of International Cooperation, the National Planning Commission of Nigeria, introduced the contribution of Nigeria's special economic zones to economic growth with respect to population, geography, regional structure and degree of marketization, and their role in poverty reduction. Unlike China, Nigeria's special economic zones gathered more capital-intensive industries. Therefore, for poverty reduction, they needed to learn the advanced experience of China on the contribution of different types of foreign capitals and different types of trade to poverty reduction in different periods of economic development.

Wan Zengwei, President of the Shanghai Pudong Institute of Reform and Development, explained the typical poverty alleviation case of Pudong from three aspects: first, the development and opening up of Pudong was also a paradigm of China's reform and opening-up—to promote work in all areas by drawing upon experience gained on key points; second, in terms of background, Pudong's development boldly explored the marketization of factors; third, Pudong was different from the Shenzhen SEZ in that it used more FDIs, which also had a positive impact on poverty reduction.

Ms. ROSINE MAWANGA, Director General of the Social Economy, Ministry of SMEs and Crafts of Gabon, introduced the ethnic composition, geographical location and resource endowment of Gabon. Due to the development of petroleum resources, the per capita income of Gabon was four times higher than that in other parts of the Sahara area, so Gabon paid more attention to poverty reduction and took corresponding measures. Three main pillars supported its poverty reduction strategies: First, cooperation with the state in environmental protection to build a green Gabon; second, development and transformation of the raw material market to build industry in Gabon; and third, building services in Gabon to increase employment opportunities and reduce the proportion of the low-income population. Moreover, Gabon was also looking forward to cooperation with Shenzhen.

Professor Li Xiaoyun, Dean of the College of Humanities and Developmental Studies of the China Agricultural University, analyzed why China could implement the reform and development and why it should establish special economic zones from the aspects of political system, social structure and cultural system, as well as the attitudes of other countries towards Africa and Africa's attitude toward other countries. From the successful experience of China's special economic zones and inspiration for Africa, Professor Li Xiaoyun pointed out that the specific national conditions and the levels of political, social and cultural development of African countries should be fully considered in order to truly achieve the economic development of Africa and the reduction of poverty.

Mr. Amare Asgedom, Head of the Bureau of Housing Development and Government Building Construction, Ministry of Urban Development and Construction of Ethiopia, introduced Ethiopia's efforts in poverty reduction and economic development, and analyzed the construction of infrastructures, the status of human capital, the political system and the process of industrialization of the country. In light of the direction of its developmental strategy, Ethiopia needed to develop agriculture for driving industrial development, which would be the basis for economic development and poverty alleviation. The raw materials, sufficient labor and electricity were advantages for Ethiopia in attracting foreign investment, and it also continuously established and improved the industrial clusters. Finally, Ethiopia's housing project achieved some success in reducing poverty, and the future challenge was how this project could benefit low- and middle-income families more.

Chen Xin, Head of the Division of Management, Suzhou Branch of the China Development Bank, with the Suzhou Industrial Park as the case, introduced the role of the China Development Bank in the development and construction of the industrial park: as a financial institution for development, the specific objectives and foundations of the bank could provide the construction of infrastructures with funds for the park; it could establish a cooperative relationship among the enterprises within the park and ensure rapid development of industrialization in the industrial park; the bank could effectively combine construction planning and investment and financing planning and provide powerful support for the industrial park; and it could be a strong signal and guide the input of social capital.

4 Responses and Ideas of Representatives from African Countries

In the seminar, the African participants indicated that they came to China to attend the seminar with the purpose of sharing and learning from experiences. For Africans, the special economic zone is still an emerging topic which they are quite interested in.

In summary of the seminar, Hailemeskel Tefera, State Minister of the Ministry of Urban Development and Construction of Ethiopia shared his experience and refined the six principles that could be learnt and taken as best practice for Africa. First, agricultural development could lead industrialization. Many African countries were agrarian countries, so the building up of industry could be realized only through agricultural development. Second, the principle of export-led industrialization, and the foreign market played a crucial role in securing a dependable market for value added agricultural products. Third, the domestic-foreign investment partnership must be established. Fourth, the private sectors should be developed and private enterprises could become an important engine of the strategy for industrial development. Fifth, the government has played a leading managerial role, but it should not intervene in the investment areas. Sixth, favorable conditions must be created for industrial development and developmental entrepreneurs. In order to enable the developmental entrepreneurs to serve as an engine of industrial development, a better enabling environment for the development of the private sector had to be facilitated.

As for the organization of this seminar, the representatives of Africa benefited a lot for their actual work on such a platform arranged by the China Center for Special Economic Zone Research of Shenzhen University for face-to-face exchanges with Chinese entrepreneurs and scholars, especially regarding the challenges and difficulties faced by Chinese enterprises in investing in Africa.

Simão Joaquim, Head of the SEZ Office, the Ministry of Planning and Development of Mozambique, pointed out that the organizers of the seminar provided such a platform for collisions and sparks of thoughts, so that participants could learn a lot about China's great achievements after nearly 30 years of reform and opening-up. In particular, African representatives could take these successful experiences back to their home countries. He also warmly invited experts and scholars from the China Center for Special Economic Zone Research of Shenzhen University to carry out research projects in Africa, and make overall planning and policy design for the development of SEZs there.

Pre Simféitchéou, Chief of Staff and Chief Economist at the Office of the Prime Minister of Togo, hoped to be "a good student when you are a student" and that during this entire seminar, African officials could learn the developmental model of China and Shenzhen and become good managers.

5   Conclusions

Representatives of the International Poverty Reduction Center in China (IPRCC) and the United Nations Development Programme (UNDP) spoke highly of the organization of this seminar and expressed their desire for further cooperation in the future.

Steven Sabey, senior policy adviser of UNDP China, expressed that "the seminar has been thoughtful in all aspects and has achieved a full range of success. Special thanks to Shenzhen University. This is the first time we have cooperated with Shenzhen University, the first time the poverty reduction center and UNDP have cooperated with Shenzhen University, but we can easily see that our seminar is particularly abundant and prolific in topics, and that the effect of the whole work is very good!"

In view of continuing to deepen cooperation and establish a network after the seminar, Sabey emphasized that exchanges between China and Africa could be continued as practice-led. "We hope that not only preparations in the past, but also in the middle of the seminar and beyond, we can continue this kind of exchange. We can continue to talk about some topics we have not discussed. That is, more information needs to be collected for successful experiences of China in this aspect and in that aspect. I hope that more seminars of this type can take place. In the future, we will host more of these seminars. This seminar is very successful and all the details are great."

Huang Chengwei, Deputy Director of the International Center for Poverty Reduction in China, stated, "Special thanks to the team of the China Center for Special Economic Zone Research of Shenzhen University for their great efforts and hard work in preparing, convening and organizing this seminar. It is the patient, meticulous and considerate arrangements of the organizers that makes this high-level meeting successful."

Generally, this seminar is of great significance for extending the international influence of "Special Economic Zones and China's Path" and demonstrating the positive developmental image of the Shenzhen Special Economic Zone and enterprises. This also coincides with the major strategic move of China's academics "going global" required by the nation, and an important approach to enhancing the influence of Chinese culture and disseminating Chinese academic achievements.

The China Center for Special Economic Zone Research hosts this type of conference for academic considerations, introduces the theoretical system of "Special Economic Zones and China's Path" into the mainstream theoretical and practical perspectives of foreign countries, and makes due contributions for deepening the understanding of China's economy, society and traditional culture, facilitating academic exchanges and dialogues between China and foreign countries and enhancing the international influence of Chinese philosophy and social sciences.

Zhang Ping Lecturer at the China Center for Special Economic Zone Research, Shenzhen University, Ph.D., with research interests in behavioral games, economic comparison and institutional analysis of Taiwan, Hong Kong and Macao SARs.